"I've read many good books on dealing with temptation but this one by Russell Moore stands out in a class by itself. I can guarantee that your spiritual health will benefit greatly from giving serious attention to this book. It will help you not only understand how temptation works, but also how to defeat it."

Rick Warren, Pastor, Saddleback Church, Lake Forest, California; author, *The Purpose Driven Life*

"In *Tempted and Tried*, Russell Moore carefully examines the sinfulness of our hearts, biblically exposes the strategies of our Adversary, and ultimately exalts the Savior who alone has conquered sin and death. Indeed, Christ is our only hope, and this book gloriously points us to him."

David Platt, Senior Pastor, The Church at Brook Hills, Birmingham, Alabama; author, *Radical: Taking Back Your Faith from the American Dream*

"Some people are incredible writers but have little to say. Others have great substance but are boring as all get out to read. Russell Moore is that rare author whose skills as a writer are matched by his theological and biblical substance. He both engages your imagination and stretches you intellectually. This man knows the Bible and he teaches it in a way that pierces the heart. Russell will not only make you think, he will make you think more biblically—an activity that is more dangerous and subversive than you would imagine.

If you're struggling with sin in some form, you might assume that reading a book called *Tempted and Tried* would be a depressing reminder of all your failings. But that is not what this book is. It is realistic and honest about sin and evil, but more than anything it gloriously sets forth Jesus as the Devil-smashing Victor that he is. It will give you hope. It will give you courage to press on. It will stir your heart to keep battling temptation in the confidence of Christ's victory. I highly recommend it."

Joshua Harris, Senior Pastor, Covenant Life Church, Gaithersburg, Maryland; author, *Dug Down Deep*

"Russell Moore has given us a book that is simultaneously theological, personal, and literary, inviting us into the story of Jesus' battle with temptation. There, we discover our own war with an enemy that is both within us and prowling around us. Instead of a formulaic approach to resisting temptation, he shows us how to look to Jesus, who accomplishes what we can't and journeys with us into our battle. Be forewarned, this book will open your eyes to temptation in ways that are sure to leave you uncomfortably alert."

Mike Cosper, Pastor of Worship and Arts, Sojourn Community Church, Louisville, Kentucky

"Russell Moore is a riveting writer, and you won't have to read this book for long before you also find out that he knows some things that you need to know about the deceitfulness of our hearts, the trials of temptation, the schemes of the Tempter, and the power and grace of the Savior. Wise beyond his years, and unashamedly supernatural and biblical in his approach, I almost hear the old Puritan Thomas Brooks speaking to me in Dr. Moore's words (albeit in a Mississippi dialect!). In one of the great hymns of the church, 'Jesus, What a Friend for Sinners,' we sing 'Tempted, tried, and sometimes failing, He, my strength, my victory wins.' But how? That's what Russell Moore shows us in this book. Read it. Search your heart. Pray for grace. And join the fight."

Ligon Duncan, Senior Minister, First Presbyterian Church,
Jackson, Mississippi; President, Alliance of Confessing Evangelicals

"Every Christian wants to turn from their sin and to the God who bore that sin. The real question is how can believers do this consistently and thoroughly? Russell Moore has come alongside our struggle to repent of sin and relish the Savior. This book is the best kind of theology: God-centered and practical. Read it as you resist temptation by worshiping Jesus who has forever defeated the Tempter."

Darrin Patrick, Lead Pastor, The Journey, St. Louis, Missouri

"With the courage and insight of Luther, the humor of Erasmus, and the spiritual insight of Spurgeon, Russell Moore in this volume, *Tempted and Tried*, accomplishes what few scholars are able to do; he brings vast learning to a table set to feed both scholars like him and the rest of us common folk also. With precise theology on a solidly biblical basis, buttressed by wide reading and profound experience, Russell Moore helps us all deal with the daily temptations of life and triumph in Christ. This volume, like C. S. Lewis' *The Screwtape Letters*, finds the follower of Jesus where he is and assists him in his climb to a higher realm. No believer serious about encountering temptation should miss this book."

Paige Patterson, President, Southwestern Baptist Theological Seminary,
Fort Worth, Texas

"Dr. Russell Moore's new book, one of the most practical I have seen in a long time, is an excellent manual of how to recognize and deal with temptation. Its prose is engaging, its biblical support solid, its illustrations lively and consistently to the point."

Patrick Henry Reardon, Pastor, All Saints' Orthodox Church,
Chicago, Illinois; author, *Christ in the Psalms*

TEMPTED AND TRIED

TEMPTED
and
TRIED

TEMPTATION
and the
TRIUMPH *of* CHRIST

Russell D. Moore

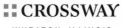
WHEATON, ILLINOIS

Tempted and Tried

Copyright © 2011 by Russell D. Moore

Published by Crossway
    1300 Crescent Street
    Wheaton, Illinois 60187

Cover design: Dual Identity inc.

Cover photo: iStock

First printing, 2011

Printed in the United States of America

Italics in biblical quotes indicate emphasis added.

Unless otherwise indicated, Scripture quotations are from the ESV® Bible (*The Holy Bible, English Standard Version*®), copyright © 2001 by Crossway. Used by permission. All rights reserved.

Scripture quotations marked KJV are from the *King James Version* of the Bible.

Scripture quotations marked NASB are from *The New American Standard Bible*˙. Copyright © The Lockman Foundation 1960, 1962, 1963, 1968, 1971, 1972, 1973, 1975, 1977. Used by permission.

Scripture references marked NIV are taken from the *Holy Bible, New International Version*˙. Copyright © 1973, 1978, 1984 Biblica. Used by permission of Zondervan. All rights reserved. The "NIV" and "New International Version" trademarks are registered in the United States Patent and Trademark Office by Biblica. Use of either trademark requires the permission of Biblica.

Scripture references marked NKJV are from *The New King James Version*. Copyright © 1982, Thomas Nelson, Inc. Used by permission.

ISBN-13: 978-1-4335-1580-4
ISBN-10: 1-4335-1580-6
PDF ISBN: 978-1-4335-1588-0
Mobipocket ISBN: 978-1-4335-1596-5
ePub ISBN: 978-1-4335-1597-2

Library of Congress Cataloging-in-Publication Data
Moore, Russell, 1971–
   Tempted and tried : temptation and the triumph of Christ / Russell D. Moore.
     p. cm.
   Includes bibliographical references and indexes.
   ISBN 978-1-4335-1580-4 (tp)
   1. Temptation. 2. Jesus Christ—Temptation. I. Title.
BT335.M66   2011
232.9'5—dc22   2010036247

Crossway is a publishing ministry of Good News Publishers.

VP		20	19	18	17	16	15	14	13	12	11
15	14	13	12	11	10	9	8	7	6	5	4	3	2

To Samuel Kenneth Moore:
God heard our prayer when we called out for you.
I pray you hear your name when he calls out to you.
(1 SAM. 1:20; 3:10)

CONTENTS

ACKNOWLEDGMENTS

I would like to say that I wrote this book out in the desert, on a forty-day trek of prayer and fasting. But that's not how it happened. Instead I went home. My family and I left the whirl of our lives in Louisville and went south to our hometown of Biloxi, Mississippi, just as the spring edged into summer. Most of this book was written there, overlooking my beloved Gulf of Mexico from a beachfront room, or listening to the clang of streetcars in the French Quarter of New Orleans. And I have to tell you that, yes, it is convicting to wipe a smudge of powdered sugar off the just-finished page on the stones-to-bread temptation, realizing that its writing was accompanied by beignets and café au lait.

For this time away, I am indebted beyond words to R. Albert Mohler Jr., president, and the board of trustees of The Southern Baptist Theological Seminary. They surprised me on my fifth anniversary as dean with this minisabbatical, and it was what I needed to get this project done. I am grateful to President Mohler and my colleagues, especially Dan Dumas, Randy Stinson, Chuck Lawless, and Don Whitney, for taking over my responsibilities while I was away, including May graduation exercises. I am also appreciative of my congregation, the Fegenbush Lane campus of Highview Baptist Church, for cheerfully giving me leave during this time.

I acknowledge my gratitude to the people I suppose would be called my "staff," although they genuinely are in every way more like kin to me: Robert Sagers, Christopher Cowan, Katy Ferguson, Phillip Bethancourt, Ruthanne McRae, and Daniel Patterson. I am particularly indebted to Robbie Sagers, my co-laborer, student, and friend, for his ongoing work on this and many other projects, and to Daniel Patterson, who edited every chapter as I finished it, and whose thoughtful comments were priceless to me.

I am thankful for the Crossway team, especially Justin Taylor, who encouraged this project from the start, and for the diligent labors of my editor, Ted Griffin.

My beautiful wife, Maria, that girl from Ocean Springs, enabled this project with her sweetness and glory as helpmate and confidant. While I was writing, she was supervising four young boys as they romped through the beachfronts and bayous of our hometown. She read each chapter as it was written, providing helpful commentary as we went. An unintended benefit of that is that I am quite sure, after her reading of chapter 1, that I will never have to run into a hotel lobby in the rain by myself again.

I am thankful to God for all four of my sons. My last book, *Adopted for Life*, was dedicated to our older sons, Benjamin and Timothy. This one is for our third, the inimitable Samuel Kenneth Moore, who as of this writing is five years old. We first "met" Samuel in what we thought were the symptoms of (another) miscarriage. Having been through this so many times before, we were almost numb to it and scheduled the customary follow-up doctor's appointment. The ultrasound there showed what we never expected to see: a beating heart. Though expecting every week of the pregnancy to lose him, to our great joy that little heart is beating still, bringing delight into our home with every morning he wakes up. Every time I see that little face, I am reminded of the meaning of his name, that our God hears.

Samuel has asked often through this project when I will be done with "the book on the Devil." He, like all of us, will meet that evil spirit of the wild places one day. My prayer for him is that when that day comes, he will hear the voice of the God of his fathers. Like our Lord Jesus, I pray Samuel discerns the voice of his God from the voice of the imposter Serpent. And I pray that my Samuel, like the prophet for whom he is named, will take up the sword of the Spirit, the Word of God hidden in his heart, and hew temptation to pieces before the Lord (1 Sam. 15:33). I pray he lives up to his name.

Tempted and tried, we're oft made to wonder
Why it should be thus all the day long,
While there are others living about us,
Never molested, though in the wrong.

Farther along we'll know all about it,
Farther along we'll understand why;
Cheer up, my brother, live in the sunshine,
We'll understand it all by and by.

SOUTHERN FOLK HYMN

1

WRESTLING WITH DEMONS

Why Temptation Matters

So there I was, standing in a hotel lobby with a strange woman, a throbbing heartbeat, and a guilty conscience. In most ways it wasn't nearly as bad as it looks typed out on this page. But in lots of ways it was even worse. I didn't really do anything wrong—and certainly didn't set out to do anything wrong. But that was just the problem. Before I knew it, I was scared at how mindless I was about the whole scenario.

I'd gotten here kind of accidentally. My family and I were driving—through the state of Tennessee, I think—when one of those sudden rainstorms had emerged, the kind that brings the slick grime right up to the surface of the road and mucks up the windshield with smearing drops the wipers can't seem to keep up with. Even though we hadn't gotten nearly as far as I'd hoped, the rain just wasn't letting up. I pulled the minivan off the highway and left my family in the vehicle while I ran in to check for a vacancy in a chain hotel whose sign we'd seen through the storm.

I waited in line at the front desk. I was exhausted and irritated, mostly because of the rain and the almost Hindu-like mantra coming from the backseat—"Dad, he's hitting me"—repeated over and over and over again. My thoughts were clicking around as I waited to check us in, moving from sermon ideas to budget numbers to parenting strategies.

The clerk, a young woman, gave an artificial pout and then a wink and a half smile, indicating she could tell it'd been a trying day. "Well, hey there," she said, and as soon as she said it I noticed she reminded me of a friend I'd known back in college. She had dimples in her cheeks, I think, and she tossed her hair back, holding it there in her hand for a minute as she checked on whether two adjoining rooms, one for my wife and me and one for the kids, would be available that night. When she called me by my first name, I felt a little jump in my stomach—like the feeling you get in the split second when the roller coaster creaks to the top of the pinnacle, just before you can see the drop in front of you. I started to ask, "How do you know my name?" before I realized she was reading my credit card.

As this woman waited for the credit card machine to rattle out my receipt and punch out my automated key, we talked about the rain outside and about how traffic was bad because of the ball game at the high school stadium down the road. She laughed at my little quips. She teased me about my soaking wet hair from running through the stormy weather. I felt like I was in college again, or maybe even in high school. I didn't have to judge between disputes over who had whose toys or explain how predestination and free will work together in the Bible. I didn't have to pay a mortgage or tell a faculty member he couldn't have a raise. And I liked it.

Just then I heard a word I never thought would terrify me, but it did, just that once. I heard "Daddy." And then I heard it again. "Daddy!" my three-year-old son Samuel cried out as he rode through the lobby in the luggage cart being pushed by his two older brothers. "Look at me!"

I did look at him and wiped a bead of sweat from my forehead as I realized I had completely forgotten that my family was waiting outside for me in the van. As I signed the credit card form, I noticed that my voice and body language toward the clerk had suddenly become a good bit more businesslike.

I felt as if I'd been caught doing something wrong, and it rattled me. As I pushed the luggage cart onto the elevator ("Benjamin, don't swing from that"; "No, Timothy, you can't have that 40-ounce Full Throttle energy drink from the vending machine"), I mentally reassured myself that everything was okay. I hadn't *done* anything; not even close. But for some reason I had paid attention to that woman, and worse, I hadn't noticed myself paying attention to her until my kids interrupted me.

Now on the one hand nothing happened. I hadn't—to use the biblical language for it—"lusted in my heart" for her. I'd just engaged in a minute of conversation. I'm afraid you'll think of me as some kind of leering, pervertlike preacher when, although I don't know all my own weaknesses, I don't think I'm particularly vulnerable at this point. I don't "check women out" as they pass by (and I roll my eyes when I see other men who do). Moreover, this woman's interest in me was nil. If she read about this, she would, I'm quite sure, not remember it. And if she did remember it, she would probably say, "You mean that little guy who looks like a cricket? Well, bless his heart."

But it scared me. I was scared not by what actually happened but by a glimpse into what could have happened. What if I hadn't been on a road trip with my family but on a business trip alone, as I often am? What if she'd been interested in me? For a moment, just a moment, I'd forgotten who I was, who I am. Husband. Pastor. Son. Christian. Daddy. I was struck by the thought, *It starts like this, doesn't it?* It starts as a series of innocent departures, gradually leading to something more and something more. What scares me even more is to wonder how many of those situations have happened in my life when I never had the clarifying moment of "waking up" to the horror around me. It scared me to think of how something like this could so seemingly naturally happen. What if I wasn't just accidentally winding up there in that hotel lobby at that exact point of exhaustion and irritability? What if I was being led?

A friend of mine heard me talk about my hotel lobby scare and pointed me to an older man in the faith who had written of a strikingly similar situation, also with his child, several years before at a restaurant. After that I've found scores of men and women who have had similar moments of terror at looking behind the veil of their own temptations. My story was not unique, and neither is yours. There's something wild out there, and something wild in here.

The Bible locates this wildness in the universal tragedy of Eden, a tragedy the Spirit locates squarely in our own psyche as well as in history. Sure enough, the canon of Scripture shows us tracks of blood from the very edge of Eden outward. The biblical story immediately veers from Paradise to depictions of murder, drunkenness, incest, gang rape, polygamy, and on and on and on, right down to whatever's going on with you. But between our cosmic story and your personal story, there's Israel's story, holding the two together.

After Eden, God unveiled some hope through the calling of a man he named Abraham, "the father of many nations" (Rom. 4:17). It was through this man's line, the ancient oracles said, that God would bless all of the nations, that he'd restore the kingdom to the earth.

This all seemed to be on the verge of happening when God rescued Abraham's descendants, dramatically and publicly, from their tyranny by the Egyptian state. But then, just as tragically as in Eden, something happened in the desert. The kingdom of priests turned out to be not as far away from the enemy as they'd thought. There was wildness in the wilderness, still.

God called a series of warrior-kings, men of great renown who would fight enemies and hold back the wild. But, again, these kings also succumbed to the wildness inside themselves—to sexual anarchy, egoism, materialism, occultism—and the kingdom collapsed, again, to the wildness outside.

Then, in the fullness of time, Jesus arrived, preaching the good news of the kingdom of God. In three of the four Gospel accounts in the New Testament, we're told of a strange experience at the beginning of Jesus' public mission in which Jesus was led by the Spirit to be tempted by the Devil (Matt. 4:1–11;

Mark 1:12–13; Luke 4:1–13). He was away from his family and followers, out in a desert place in Judea; literally, he was in "the wilderness" or "the wild places."

He went out there to meet his ancestors' ancient foe—and ours—and to undo what had been done. If you will ever see the kingdom of God, it will be because of what happened under that desert moon, where the kingdoms approached each other, surveyed each other, and, long time coming, attacked each other.

Somehow the evil spirit of Eden appeared to Jesus. Poets and artists have speculated for centuries on what this must have looked or felt like. Did Jesus, like Eve before him, see the figure of a snake out there in the desert? Did Satan appear, as the apostle Paul warned us he could, as a glorious "angel of light" (2 Cor. 11:14)? Did he appear, as some icons and paintings depict, as a hideous goatlike monster bearing a tantalizing morsel in his hoof? Or did the Devil manifest himself, as he most often does to us, invisibly but with the painfully personal suggestiveness that disguises itself as one's own thoughts? The Gospels don't tell us. They simply tell us the Devil was there, and he was not silent.

Almost every world religion—and almost every backwater cult—has sensed that there are spiritual beings out there in the universe, including evil superintelligent beings that mean us harm. The gospel of Jesus Christ directly confronts this dark reality—in a way that often makes us contemporary Western people squirm.

In the beginning pages of Scripture, we are introduced to a cryptic hyperintelligent snake (Gen. 3:1), a being later identified as a dragon (Revelation 12), the chief of a race of rebel beings engaged in guerrilla warfare against the Most High God. These beings have sometimes been called "the Watchers." Sometimes people have called them "gods." Sometimes they're called "demons" or "devils." The Bible often calls them "rulers" or "principalities" and "powers." The Christian church has confessed from the beginning that an old monster, known by many names but identified in the Bible as Satan, governs these creatures. How could a creature formed by a good deity become so twisted into a monstrosity? That's not our story, and the Scripture doesn't tell us. The Bible describes evil, ultimately, as "the mystery of lawlessness" (2 Thess. 2:7), and we really shouldn't poke about too much in what we cannot comprehend.

In order for Jesus to proclaim the kingdom of God, he needed also to point out why the world that God created was anything other than his kingdom anyway. Jesus, like the prophets before him, showed us that the cosmic order was hijacked millennia ago by these "rulers" and "authorities" (Eph. 6:12). Jesus in his taking on of our nature, offering himself up in death as a sacrifice for our sins, and turning back the curse of death in his resurrection, has ended the claim these demonic powers have on the universe. These powers don't want to give up their dark reign, so they are lashing back, and with fury. This means war.

The sheer animal force of temptation ought to remind us of something: the universe is demon haunted. It also ought to remind us there's only one among us who has ever wrestled the demons and prevailed.

The temptations of Jesus in the desert show us what kind of strategies the powers will use on us. While I was writing this book, I heard an elderly pastor reflect that over half of the confessions of sin he hears from people these days were physically impossible when he started his ministry. There's a lot of truth to that. Saint Augustine never had to counsel, as I have, a wife whose husband has decided he wants to be a woman. Thomas Aquinas didn't have to speak to the issue of compulsive electronic gaming. And the list could go on and on.

But none of these are new temptations, just newer ways of surrendering to old temptations. The temptations themselves are, as the Scripture puts it, "common to man" (1 Cor. 10:13), and in Jesus' desert testing we see how true this is. Here the Scriptures identify for us the universal strategies of temptation. You will be tempted exactly as Jesus was, because Jesus was being tempted exactly as we are. You will be tempted with consumption, security, and status. You will be tempted to provide for yourself, to protect yourself, and to exalt yourself. And at the core of these three is a common impulse—to cast off the fatherhood of God.

As we'll discuss later, God's fatherhood is embedded in pictures we see all around us in the creation order, especially in our human nature. In some ways a human father is, essentially, a second parent, doing some of the same functions and callings as a mother in the raising of children. But there are important distinctions, too, in most human cultures' understanding of what it means to be a father. Most human peoples have seen fathers as bearing a unique role in provision, protection, and the passing on of an inheritance (whether through a literal inheritance or simply through the role modeling of what it means to make a future for oneself).[1] This isn't to say that fathers—or biological parents—are the exclusive carriers of those roles. It is only to say that these archetypes of fatherhood, expressing themselves in various ways, show up repeatedly in human civilization. Some would attribute this to evolutionary natural selection. I would argue, instead, that this ideal of fatherhood persists because of something distinctively true about the fatherhood of God in his care, discipline, and husbandry of his creation and his creatures.

Temptation is so strong in our lives precisely because it's not about us. Temptation is an assault by the demonic powers on the rival empire of the Messiah. That's why conversion to Christ doesn't diminish the power of temptation—as we often assume—but actually, counterintuitively, ratchets it up. If you bear the Spirit of the One the powers rage against, they will seek to tear down the icon of the Crucified they see embedded in you (1 Pet. 4:14; Rev. 12:17). Ultimately, the agony of temptation is not about you or me. We're targeted because we resemble Jesus, our firstborn brother. We all, whether believers or not, bear some resemblance to Jesus because we share with him a human nature in the image of God. As we come to find peace with God through Jesus, though, we begin a journey of being conformed more and more into the image of Christ (Rom. 8:29). The demons shriek in the increasing glory of that light, and they'll seek even more frenetically to put it out of their sight.

When I say that we share common temptations, don't get me wrong. I am not saying that we all experience this temptation in precisely the same way. You may never find yourself in the situation I did in the hotel lobby, or anything like it. I don't know what's wrong with you. Maybe you tear up when you think about the words you screamed at your kids this morning. Maybe you've deleted the history cache of your computer this week, promising yourself you'll never access those images again. Maybe you carry that empty snack bag with you in your purse to throw away later so the people in your office won't see it in the wastebasket. Maybe the prescription drugs in your desk drawer right now are the only things keeping you sane, but you fear they're making you crazy. Maybe you just can't stop thinking about the smell of your coworker's hair or the clink of the whiskey glass at the table nearby.

Maybe what you're tempted to do is so wild that my publisher wouldn't allow me to print it here, or maybe it's so tame that I wouldn't even think to mention it. I don't know. But I think I know what's behind it all.

You are being tempted right now, and so am I. Most of the time we don't even know it. And in every one of those moments we want either to overestimate or underestimate the power of that temptation. We overestimate it by thinking something along the lines of, "I have these feelings, so therefore I'm predestined to be this kind of person." We underestimate it by thinking something along the lines of, "I'm not tempted to do anything terrible—like adultery or murder. I'm just struggling with this small thing—bitterness over my infertility."

The gospel, though, brings good news to tempted rebels like us. Just as our temptation is part of a larger story, so is our exit strategy from its power. The same Spirit who led Jesus through the wilderness and empowered him to overcome the Evil One now surges through all of us who are joined by faith to Jesus. We overcome temptation the same way he did, by trusting in our Father and hearing his voice.

The danger we face presently isn't cognitive but primal. The demons are thinkers. They know who God is, and they tremble before that truth (James 2:19). Mere intellect cannot ensure that we are "led not into temptation" or "delivered from evil." Only "faith working through love" (Gal. 5:6) can do that. We are not simply overcoming something about human psychology. We're wrestling against the cosmic powers (Eph. 6:12), grappling with an animal-like spirit intent on devouring us (1 Pet. 5:8).

This isn't a self-help guide, promising to do for temptation what a diet manual promises to do for obesity. Some of you reading this now will recognize the good news of what's written here, and you'll abandon it all for an orgasm or an ego. But maybe some of you who believe yourselves to be freaks of nature will cast that burden off as you see a Christ who identified himself with you even in temptation. Ask for what you want, and you'll find what you're looking for (Matt. 7:7–8).

Times like this call for the kind of desperation that ought to drive us to the only place we can find refuge—the spike-scabbed arms of Jesus of Nazareth. "Tempted and tried, we're oft made to wonder," the old gospel song says, "why it should be thus all the day long." This book won't remove the mystery of iniquity, but I pray it will rekindle the wonder. Before we can see what's really going on in the wilderness out there—and in the wilderness in our own hearts—we'll have to listen, again, to "the beginning of the gospel of Jesus Christ, the Son of God" (Mark 1:1).

At the core of the gospel message is Jesus, who was tempted and tried in every way we are but who was never anything but triumphant. He is a high priest who shares our nature, who can pray for us and with us. He is, as God announced right before his testing, the "beloved Son" of God. But he is not by himself. He is "the firstborn," to be sure, but he is "the firstborn among many brothers" (Rom. 8:29). Because we have a sympathetic High Priest, tempted in every way as we are, we are able then "with confidence [to] draw near to the throne of grace, that we may receive mercy and find grace to help in time of need" (Heb. 4:16). And what are we to pray? "Your kingdom come, your will be done. . . . Lead us not into temptation, but deliver us from evil" (Matt. 6:9–13 NIV).

Quite simply, following Jesus isn't just a metaphor. His first disciples literally "followed" after him all across the map of first-century Palestine. Jesus told them, "Where I am going you cannot follow me now, but you will follow afterward" (John 13:36). He says the same to all of us who have recognized him in the two thousand years since. We will "suffer with him in order that we may also be glorified with him" (Rom. 8:17). This "suffering" the Bible speaks of isn't only political persecution or social marginalization or difficult circumstances, as we often tend to think. It is also the suffering of temptation, as God walks us through the place of the powers.

Author Barbara Brown Taylor recounts going to a seminar where a presenter talked about taking student groups out into the wilderness to experience in hiking and rafting "the untamed holiness of the wild." Brown writes that a participant raised his hand and asked whether "there are predators in those places who are above you on the food chain." The wilderness guide said that there weren't, of course, because he wouldn't take his students to a place where they would be so jeopardized. "I wouldn't either," the audience member replied, "but don't lull them into thinking that they have experienced true wilderness. It's only wilderness if there's something out there that can eat you."[2] There's some wisdom there. For Jesus, there was something dark and ancient and predatory out there in the desert.

Where we join Jesus in temptation won't usually look as scary to us. We'll meet our temptations in a hotel lobby or at the breakfast table or in the break room at work. But it's just as wild and just as perilous. And there, in a thousand different places, we will face temptation in every one of the ways Jesus first faced it in that demon-haunted wasteland. If we have eyes to see, we'll recognize that we're wandering toward the desert place even now. The Spirit will take us through the same path he took with our Elder Brother, right through the place of the Devil's reign. But we are not there by accident, and we are not alone.

2

SLAUGHTERHOUSE DRIVE

*Why You're on the Verge of Wrecking Your Life
(Especially If You Don't Know It)*

There was something rhythmic, almost soothing about the soft clatter of it all. The soothing repetition sounded kind of like a summer thunderstorm coming up from the coast or a rickety old midnight train off in the distance. I had no idea that what I was listening to was the rhythm of cattle marching to a slaughterhouse. It turns out what I'd happened upon, kind of randomly driving in my car, was a public radio program about factory farming. The broadcast was about how to kill cows, but with kindness.[1]

Actually, it wasn't really about the cows. They were just sort of the backdrop. The segment instead profiled a highly functioning autistic scientist who had learned through years of research how to register which stimuli produce which animal sounds and how to track what scares or stresses livestock. It turns out that the beef industry was willing to pay for this information, and not entirely due to their humanitarian goals. High stress levels in animals can release hormones that could downgrade the quality of the meat.

Some of the largest corporations in the world hired this

scientist to visit their meat plants with a checklist. She said her secret was the insight that novelty distresses cows. A slaughter-house, then, in order to keep the cattle relaxed, should remove anything from the sight of the animals that isn't completely familiar. The real problem is novelty. "If dairy cattle are used to seeing bright yellow raincoats slung over gates every day when they enter the milking parlor, there'd be no problem," she counsels. "It's the animal who's seeing a bright yellow raincoat slung over a gate for the first time at a slaughter plant or feedlot who's going to balk."[2]

Workers shouldn't yell at the cows, she said, and they should never ever use cattle prods, because they are counter-productive and unneeded. If you just keep the cows contented and comfortable, they'll go wherever they're led. Don't surprise them, don't unnerve them, and above all, don't hurt them (well, at least until you slit their throats at the end).

Along the way, this scientist devised a new technology that has revolutionized the ways of the big slaughter operations. In this system the cows aren't prodded off the truck but are led, in silence, onto a ramp. They go through a "squeeze chute," a gentle pressure device that mimics a mother's nuzzling touch. The cattle continue down the ramp onto a smoothly curving path. There are no sudden turns. The cows experience the sen-sation of going home, the same kind of way they've traveled so many times before.

As they mosey along the path, they don't even notice when their hooves are no longer touching the ground. A conveyor belt slowly lifts them gently upward, and then, in the twin-kling of an eye, a blunt instrument levels a surgical strike right between their eyes. They're transitioned from livestock to meat, and they're never aware enough to be alarmed by any of it. The pioneer of this technology commends it to the slaughterhouses and affectionately gives it a nickname. She calls it "the stairway to heaven."

Jesus knew, long before the meat industry, that livestock are better led by voice than by prod (John 10:3). And Jesus knew that the leading voice must be familiar, not novel; gentle, not yelling. Alarmed livestock run (John 10:5). Jesus also knew these principles don't apply just to farmed animals but to human beings as well. This is why, picking up on the prophets before him, he used the imagery of humanity in general and Israel in particular as sheep, a flock needing feeding and protection and direction. Jesus likewise warned there would be those who would "shepherd" in a way that leads to death.

Here's what this has to do with your temptation. Sometimes the Bible uses the language of predator and prey to describe the relationship between tempter and tempted, but often the Scripture also speaks of temptation in the language of rancher and livestock. You are not just being tracked down—you are also being cultivated (e.g., Ezekiel 34; Zechariah 11; John 10). Those headed toward judgment are spoken of as lambs led to the slaughter (e.g., Ps. 44:22; Jer. 5:26; 50:17).

Perhaps the most striking biblical use of this imagery is found in the book of Proverbs. A father describes for his son the slow progression of a sexual tryst. The reader is given an almost aerial view of the scene, as the son wanders closer and closer to the edge of temptation (Prov. 7:6–21). The father says this is like a bird being trapped or an ox being led to the slaughter (Prov. 7:22–23). Later the book pleads with the wise to rescue those who are "stumbling to the slaughter" (Prov. 24:11). The path of temptation is gradual and intelligent, not as sudden and random as it seems.

Jesus' brother James knew the language of the slaughterhouse. A Christian bishop in Jerusalem soon after the dawn of the church, James warned the rich and contented of his day that living in "luxury and in self-indulgence" couldn't rescue them. "You have fattened your hearts in a day of slaughter," he thundered (James 5:5). James knew this partly from personal experience. He hadn't always been a holy man. As a kid he'd probably laughed at his brother—just like the rest of his kin and neighbors—as a delusional egotist at best, a demon-possessed cultist at worst. But he came to see his brother as something very different—as the express image of God and as the rightful ruler of the universe.

James knew what it was like to live in an illusion, and what it was like to wake from it. He warned the little Christian assemblies dotting the landscape in the generation after Jesus' resurrection that they would need a supernatural kind of spiritual wisdom in order to see where temptation lurks and to recognize the path it takes (James 1:5). The awful truth is that we are fallen creatures, and as such are in constant danger of being "lured" (James 1:14). Temptation—for the entire human race, for the people of Israel, and for each of us personally—starts with a question of identity, moves to a confusion of the desires, and ultimately heads to a contest of futures. In short, there's a reason you want what you don't want to want. Temptation is embryonic, personality specific, and purpose directed.

Something is afoot out there that's deeper and older and scarier than we can contemplate. The Christian Scriptures propose an answer to the question, What's wrong with me? Before you wrestle with the temptation in your own life, you'll need to see the horror of what it really is, as well as the glory of how Jesus triumphs over it. Jesus walked through the cycle of temptation for us, and does so with us. Like "a lamb that is led to the slaughter" (Isa. 53:7), he walked out into the wilderness and onto the stairway to hell.

WHO ARE YOU?

The first step in the cycle of temptation is the question of your identity. James told the poor and the beaten down to "boast in his exaltation" and told the prosperous and the up-and-coming to glory "in his humiliation" (James 1:9–10). Why? James understood that temptation begins with an illusion about the self—a skewed vision of who you are. The satanic powers don't care if your illusion is one of personal grandiosity or of self-loathing, as long as you see your current circumstance, rather than the gospel, as the eternal statement of who you are. If the poor sees his poverty as making it impossible for him to have dignity, he is fallen. If the rich sees his wealth as a denial that "like a flower of the grass he will pass away," even "in the midst of his pursuits" (James 1:10–11), then he is undone.

Temptation has always started here, from the very beginning of the cosmic story. When the Bible reveals the ancestral fall of the human race, it opens with a question of identity. The woman in the Genesis narrative was approached by a mysterious serpent, a "beast of the field" that was "more crafty" than any of the others (Gen. 3:1). And that's just the point. The woman, Eve, and her husband were created in the image of God (Gen. 1:26–27). They were living signs of God's dominion over everything except God and one another. This dominion was exhaustive, right down to "every creeping thing that creeps on the earth" (Gen. 1:26).

But here she was being interrogated by a "beast of the field" that questioned God's commands and prerogatives. Without even a word, the serpent led the woman to act as though he had dominion over her instead of the other way around. He persuaded her to see herself as an animal instead of as what she had been told she was—the image-bearing queen of the universe, a principality and power over the beasts.

At the same time the serpent was treating his queen as a fellow animal, he also subtly led her to see herself as more than an empress—as a goddess. He auditioned her for her role as deity by leading her to act like a god, distinguishing autonomously between good and evil, deciding when she and her fellow were ready for maturity, evaluating the claims of God himself. The snake prompted her to eat the fruit of the tree God had forbidden to her. The tree somehow carried within it the power to awaken the conscience to "the knowledge of good and evil" (Gen. 2:17). The serpent walked the woman along to where she could see herself as if she were the ultimate cosmic judge, free from the scrutiny of her Creator's holiness. At the very beginning of the human story was a question: Who are you?

The same is true when God started his redemption plan

by forming a new people, a tribe from the line of Abraham through whom he promised to save the world. The story of Israel opened with a temptation narrative too. *Israel*, after all, is a name that started with one man, the grandson of Abraham, and it means "God wrestler." Jacob wasn't to be the father of a great nation; that calling was reserved for his slightly older twin brother, Esau.

Jacob became the father of Israel because he tricked his brother into exchanging his birthright, his inheritance, for a meal. As with the temptation of Eve, the Bible prefaces this act with a questioning of identity. From the start, Esau was foreshadowed for ominous things. He was born red and covered with hair—like an animal—and was thus given a name that means "red." Both the animalistic appearance and the red color would show up, in horror, later in his life. Esau was born to be the firstborn, to be trained toward the responsibility of leading the tribe. He is defined in the Genesis text as a "hunter" (Gen. 25:27), and this identity that would follow him all the days of his life is further defined: he was trained to be a hunter for his father.

His father loved Esau, the Bible says, "because he ate of his game" (Gen. 25:28). The father is using Esau like a favorite bird dog, to scare up whatever it is he loves to eat. Isaac is not here modeling a provider-father, training up his son to provide for his own children. He is a consumer father, using his son to feed his own stomach, a pattern that will continue right up to the old man's death, when his dying request is for some of the boy's kill. This is not how it was supposed to be.

Jesus walked into both of those stories, and into ours. "Then Jesus was led up by the Spirit into the wilderness to be tempted by the devil," the Gospel accounts tell us (Matt. 4:1). The fourth-century Christian leader John Chrysostom was right to note that the word "then" is crucially significant here.[3] It is only "then" that Jesus went into the desert—that is, after his identity was publicly marked out by his Father. In order to understand the temptations of Jesus, we have to understand that Jesus' hair was still wet when he stepped out into the desert.

The Scriptures tell us that Jesus started his public ministry by finding his cousin, a prophet named John who was baptizing out in the wilderness, and requesting baptism. That probably sounds fairly predictable and noncontroversial, if you think of baptism as simply a religious ritual. But it's much more than that. If you had watched from the hillside, you might have noticed a long awkward conversation as the prophet and his cousin seemed to be discussing something—no, debating something. The baptizer was waving his hands, shrugging his shoulders, but then he stopped and walked with his cousin out into the river. What you would have seen is what the Gospels record as John reluctantly doing what Jesus asked him to do—to baptize him.

John's dismayed confusion is entirely appropriate. This baptism is, after all, a sign of God's judgment. That's why it is about repentance. Those "vipers" coming down to the river have been "warned" of the "wrath to come" (Matt. 3:7). By going through the water, they're acknowledging that they deserve God's winnowing fire at the Day of Judgment. As they are cleansed beneath the river, they are calling out with "an appeal to God for a good conscience" (1 Pet. 3:21), that they might be saved when the flood of his anger falls. To hear Jesus' request to be baptized would have felt to John the way it would feel to you to hear your spouse announce an interest in being listed on a registry of child molesters. Yet it was necessary, Jesus told him, "to fulfill all righteousness" (Matt. 3:15). Jesus wasn't disputing John's assessment of his identity; he was confirming it. He was indeed the Lamb of God who would take away the sins of the world by bearing them on himself. Jesus was saying to John, in effect, "You can't understand who I am without understanding who my God is, that's true; but you also can't understand who I am without understanding who my people are."

As you observed the scene, you would have noticed a tumult run through the crowd as the cousins came up out of the water.

A strange presence would have shot down from somewhere above you—what you would later be told was the Holy Spirit coming down, like a dove, on this Jesus (Matt. 3:16). Even more astounding, there would be a thunderous voice coming from the skies announcing, "This is my beloved Son, with whom I am well pleased" (Matt. 3:17).

It is impossible to understand the temptations without seeing the baptism. Water is wild. Your body is made mostly of it, and you need it to live, but it can drown you. It can sweep away your life in a flood. In the early moments of creation, we're told that the "formless and void" wild earth was covered with water, "and the Spirit of God was moving over the surface of the waters" (Gen. 1:2 NASB). The image the Bible most often uses for unpredictable danger is that of the sea, a sea the Scripture promises will give up its dead and will be no more in the coming kingdom (Rev. 21:1).

Here, in the water, Jesus identified himself with us, and God identified himself with Jesus. In every one of the temptations, Satan attempted to counteract God's voice at this point: "If you are the son of God, then . . ." This is the equivalent of the Edenic "Has God really said?" The baptism was an inauguration of Jesus' kingship, and it was a declaration of war.

Jesus, God's voice said, was "beloved" and "Son." That was who he was (and is). So what does it mean, for him and for you, that Jesus is the "Son of God"? Before we follow Jesus into the desert, we have to answer that question.

We know from the Bible that a child learns who he or she is in relation to his or her father. That's why persons in the scriptural story are known as "Joshua the son of Nun" or "John son of Zebedee." Our personal identities are shaped after a cosmic pattern, a Father from whom fatherhood in heaven and on earth is named (Eph. 3:14–15). We reflect a Father-Son dynamic in which a Father God announced, "You are my Son; today I have begotten you" (Ps. 2:7).

Jesus' sonship isn't just about the truth that he is of the same nature as God (although that's certainly true). His sonship includes his humanity. Luke, particularly, emphasizes this. Right in the middle of the story—between the baptism and the temptations—Luke recounts Jesus' genealogy, tracing his ancestors in the typical biblical fashion—"the son of . . . the son of . . . the son of . . . the son of . . . "—right back to Adam. Adam is not, though, the end of the genealogy. Adam was "the son of God" (Luke 3:38).

Because Jesus' mission was to restore the world to the way God intended it, under the rule of men and women who themselves are under the rule of Christ, Jesus must live out a life as both the ruled (under his Father's lordship) and the ruler (with dominion over everything under his feet). In order to do this, the eternal Word took on flesh (a human nature) and everything this entails. Jesus was not just a human nature; he was a human being. He was a man. He was the Son of God.

At the baptism Jesus also identified himself particularly with God's covenant people, the nation of Israel. And the Bible also refers to Israel as "son of God." In the most significant moment in Israel's history as a nation, their God, revealing himself through the prophet Moses, quarreled with Pharaoh, the king of Egypt, about Pharaoh's treatment of God's son.

Israel, of course, was nothing more at the time than a fast-multiplying band of Hebrew slaves, unnoticed by the empire except in fear that their procreation might lead to slave revolts and, with them, the collapse of an economy based on unpaid human labor. And Pharaoh himself exercised power because he was believed to be the son of a god.

With God's words in his mouth, Moses said to the Egyptian tyrant, "Thus says the LORD, 'Israel is my firstborn son, and I say to you, 'Let my son go that he may serve me'" (Ex. 4:22–23). When the ruler refused to let the Hebrews go from his domain, God retaliated by striking dead the firstborn sons of all the Egyptians, including that of Pharaoh (Ex. 4:23; 12:29–30).

God demonstrated who his son was by leading Israel safely through the waters of the sea, waters that he brought down on Pharaoh's armies in drowning judgment. The apostle Paul

called this passing through the waters the 'baptism' of Israel
(1 Cor. 10:2). Like the repentant sinners going beneath the
waters with John, Israel was brought through God's wrath
and out to the other side. God furthermore marked out his
son with a visible sign of his presence—a cloud above them
by daylight and a fire above them by night. This event was the
perpetual reminder to Israel—and to her enemies—of Israel's
identity before God. "When Israel was a child, I loved him,"
God announced, "and out of Egypt I called my son" (Hos. 11:1).

Israel experienced such a "baptism" not only at their exit
from slavery but also at their entrance into the land they were
promised. God told Moses' successor, Joshua, "Today I will begin
to exalt you in the sight of all Israel, that they may know that,
as I was with Moses, so I will be with you" (Josh. 3:7). He does
so by parting the waters of the Jordan River for Joshua, just as
he had done with the Red Sea for Moses.

At the Jordan River, John the Baptizer warned the crowds
about coming judgment by calling them away from their confidence in their ethnic identity. "And do not begin to say to yourselves, 'We have Abraham as our father,'" John preached. "For I
tell you, God is able from these stones to raise up children for
Abraham" (Luke 3:8). The issue, John reminded the masses, was
that Israel was not a matter merely of ethnic bloodline.

Abraham, after all, had been Abram, a Gentile from what
is now Iraq, before God's voice declared him to be Abraham,
"the father of many nations." Those who followed after idols,
as Hosea said had happened with God's son Israel (Hos. 11:2),
would not inherit the blessings of God. They would be disinherited, even as a fruitless tree is axed down and thrown into
the fire (Luke 3:9).

Jesus at the waters recapitulates the history of Israel. As in
the exodus, he bears the verbal announcement of identification by God, is brought through the waters of judgment, and
sees a visible demonstration from the sky of God's presence
with him. As Israel did in the conquest, he goes through the
water in order to face his enemies and, ultimately, receive his

inheritance. His name is Jesus, literally in the original Hebrew language, Joshua. And the river he comes to is the Jordan. He is the Son of God.

Finally, the "Son of God" language refers to Jesus as the rightful king of Israel and ultimately of the nations. As we've seen before with Pharaoh, it was not uncommon for an ancient ruler to declare himself a "son" of whatever god he served. God used the language of "son" for the One who would occupy the throne. He promised David concerning David's royal heir, "I will be to him a father, and he shall be to me a son" (2 Sam. 7:14). God promised that the king would be "the firstborn, the highest of the kings of the earth" (Ps. 89:27).

Throughout the history of Israel, the king's sonship was displayed in announcing him as God's man by a prophetic authority, in his anointing by that prophetic authority, and in his bearing of the Holy Spirit. David, for instance, was recognized by Saul as king, had oil poured upon his head in anointing, and received the Spirit. Even though Saul still retained the title of king—and the wealth and the entourage and the concubines— God had rejected him as Israel's monarch. The office was there, but the Holy Spirit was gone, replaced by terrorizing evil spirits instead.

At his baptism Jesus is shown to be David's long-awaited heir. The prophet—John who is in the spirit of the prophet Elijah—is there to recognize his selection by God. But instead of anointing and announcing through a prophetic go-between, God's voice directly announces Jesus as the royal Son and anoints him with the Holy Spirit himself. He was the Son of God.

Now what does Jesus' sonship, declared by baptism, have to do with whatever you're drawn toward right now? In his baptism Jesus identified himself with you, and God identified himself with Jesus. Here was a new man, a new Israel, a new king—a new start. That's why the serpent wanted to question his identity, as he questioned ours in the garden and yours wherever you are. But Jesus just stood there, in the water, unashamed before his God and, as we'll see, unashamed to be your brother.

Where Adam and Eve had cringed in hiding when they heard the sound of God walking in the garden, this man stands, unashamed, before the voice of his Father. Where Israel had trembled in the desert in front of the glowing mountain, begging not to hear the voice of God (Ex. 20:19), Jesus stands, unafraid, before his Father's voice. Unlike them, bearing as they did the shame of the satanic curse, this man has nothing to hide. His Father is well pleased with him. But the first question the Devil asked was a hidden one, wrapped up in the first clause of an offer: "If you are the son of God . . ."

This is precisely the opening salvo the demonic powers launch to this very day. The factory farm wants the cows to see themselves as pets or as companions, or as simply "free" and alone. What they don't want the cattle to recognize is that they are future meat. Identity confusion is the reason people are able to affirm one thing and do another. And it's the reason more worldview training on how to think like a Christian doesn't stop people from wrecking their lives.

Most people don't "choose" fiery tempers or alcoholic binges or torturing prisoners of war or exploiting Third-World workers or dumping toxic chemicals into their community's water supply. Most people don't first conclude that adultery is right and then start fantasizing about their neighbor swinging from a stripper pole. Most people don't first learn to praise gluttony and then start drizzling bacon grease over their second helping of chicken-fried steak. It happens in reverse.

First, you do what you want to do, even though you "know God's decree that those who practice such things deserve to die," and only then do you "give approval to those who practice them" (Rom. 1:32). You start to see yourself as either special or as hopeless, and thus the normal boundaries don't seem to apply.

It might be that you are involved in certain patterns right now and that you would, if asked, be able to tell me exactly why they are morally and ethically wrong. It's not that you are deficient in the cognitive ability to diagnose the situation. It's instead that you slowly grow to believe that your situation is exceptional ("I am a god"), and then you find all kinds of reasons why this technically isn't theft or envy or hatred or fornication or abuse of power or whatever ("I am able to discern good and evil"). Or you believe you are powerless before what you want ("I am an animal") and can therefore escape accountability ("I will not surely die"). You've forgotten who you are. You are a creature. You are also a king or a queen. You are not a beast, and you are not a god. That issue is where temptation begins.

If you had stood there by the Jordan River, watching the scene at the baptism of Jesus, you might have braced yourself for a shock wave of glory. After all, the God of Israel had just unveiled—publicly, audibly, visually—his promised Messiah. The villagers around you might have been chattering about great things—the overthrow of Rome, the throne of David, shock and awe. You might have waited to watch this new king unleash his Spirit power. Instead, though, you would see him shake out the water from his hair, pause and look at the mud on the bank, and then walk off toward the desert. As he passed by you, you might have heard him whisper to himself, something about crushing a snake's skull. Jesus knows who he is. So who do you think you are?

WHAT DO YOU WANT?

The second step in temptation is the confusion of desires. James of Jerusalem told his flock that they'd certainly face the sting of temptation and that they'd be tempted to blame it on God. "Let no one say when he is tempted, 'I am being tempted by God,'" James wrote, "for God cannot be tempted with evil, and he himself tempts no one" (James 1:13). This probably doesn't seem like a problem for you. Reader, I doubt you would ever say, "I just feel that God is entrapping me to leave for Acapulco with a fake ID and my company's retirement funds in small unmarked bills."

But the danger is that we might see our temptations as a normal part of the fabric of the universe, as the way things are supposed to be. That's true for both believers and unbelievers. We must recognize that "each person is tempted when he is lured and enticed by his own desire" (James 1:14). The human story, after all, starts with a man who blames God ("the woman whom you gave to be with me," Gen. 3:12) for the fact that he fell to his own twisted desires.

When God created humanity, he didn't design us to be blank and passionless. There was a mission to undertake, a mission that required certain drives. In order to live, we must have a drive to eat. In order to be fruitful and multiply, we must have a drive to copulate. In order to subdue the earth, there must be a drive for creativity. That's all perfectly—and I mean, literally, perfectly—human.

When the serpent attacked Eve, he did so by appealing to desires that God had created within her, desires that were, in and of themselves, like the rest of creation: "very good" (Gen. 1:31). Eve was designed to long for that which is "good for food" (Gen. 3:6) because God had created a savory array of foods in the trees around her to eat. She was designed to recognize beauty. After all, the text leading up to the temptation account celebrates the beauty of the creation, describing the majesty of the universe and the lushness of the garden in lyrical detail. It's no accident then that she is lured along by the fact that the forbidden fruit was "a delight to the eyes" (Gen. 3:6). She was designed to want to be wise, to be like God. She was, after all, crafted in God's image and was to represent him in ruling the creation as God does, by wisdom (Prov. 8:22–31). Is it any wonder she found it tempting that the fruit could make her wise?

The snake knew not to question the goodness or the sovereignty of God outright, at first. Instead he let her ponder what she wanted, and then ponder why she didn't have it. He pulled her craving along to envy and her envy along to action. Lured by her own desires, she became the serpent's slave.

A similar account is found in Israel's first temptation narrative. The story of Jacob and Esau climaxes in the perfect orchestration of events (perfect from a demonic vantage point, that is). Esau, the firstborn, was "exhausted" and starving after coming in from the fields, when he approached his brother Jacob cooking some "red stew" over a pot near the tents. "Let me eat some of that red stew, for I am exhausted," Esau barked (Gen. 25:30).

Now this was hardly what most of you would consider alluring. If you were to smell this—probably a combination of goat meat and lentils—you might have to suppress the urge to vomit. Even for Esau, this was probably fairly pedestrian fare. It was not the delicacy of the meat he'd gone into the woods to track down. But in his weakness he craved it more than anything—and by anything, at this point, I mean literally "any thing."

Everything seemed so matter-of-fact, even in the machine-gun style in which the narrative ends: ". . . and he ate and drank and rose and went his way. Thus Esau despised his birthright" (Gen. 25:34). It was just a moment, as long as it takes a famished hunter to gobble down the red stuff. He was lured away by his desires, lured to death.

Now when we consider how Jesus walked into the conflict for our desires, we must remember James's warning not to confuse temptation with God's action. That seems kind of hard to do, though, since the Scripture clearly tells us Jesus was "led" into the wilderness by the Spirit "to be tempted by the devil" (Matt. 4:1).

Is God leading Jesus into temptation? Isn't that precisely what Jesus taught us to pray against: "Lead us not into temptation"? Doesn't it seem as though God and Satan are linked in some common endeavor against a common enemy, Jesus? God forbid. Jesus was both tempted and tried.

Here in the desert we see in narrative form precisely what James taught about the nature of temptation. We are not—and

Jesus is not—tempted by God (James 1:13). To be tempted is to be enticed toward evil. "God is light, and in him is no darkness at all" (1 John 1:5). We are, however—and Jesus joins us in this—tested by God. James wrote, "Blessed is the man who remains steadfast under trial, for when he has stood the test he will receive the crown of life" (James 1:12). The difference between testing and tempting is no trivial matter. The goal of tempting is evil; the goal of testing is "that you may be perfect and complete, lacking in nothing" (James 1:4).

The ancient book of Job gives us some insight into the interplay between God's testing and Satan's tempting. The text tells us of a righteous man who is living in the fear of his God. Satan, after "going to and fro on the earth, and . . . walking up and down on it," approached God in the heavenly places to accuse Job of obedience based only on self-interest. Job's God allowed Satan to come after the man, but only to a God-decreed boundary: Satan could not take his life (Job 1:6–2:10). Satan, seeking to incite Job to curse God, intended evil. God, seeking to demonstrate the integrity of his servant, intended righteousness.

The apostle Paul recounts a similar scenario when he writes to the church at Corinth about a mysterious thorn in the flesh that plagued him. Paul said this was "a messenger of Satan to harass me" (2 Cor. 12:7). But Paul also wrote that this satanic burden was to keep him from "becoming conceited because of the surpassing greatness of the revelations" he had been given. Did the apostle mean that Satan, who is by definition a force of pride and self-exaltation, wished to sanctify Paul by cultivating his humility? No. But what Satan meant for evil, God worked together for good (Gen. 50:20; Acts 2:23–24; 4:27–28; Rom. 8:28). God's testing and Satan's tempting may coincide in the same event, but they are radically different, with different motives and different intended outcomes. In the desert Satan sought to subdue Jesus' desires, that he might condemn the world. Jesus' Father had in mind something else entirely.

We've already seen what the satanic powers have done to lure away humanity in general from God's reign. That's our universal human story. Jesus reorders human desire by join-ing the race as a desiring human being. After all, part of what binds the human race to the wicked is that in our fallen state our desires mirror those of Satan. Who Jesus is must be tested by what he wants.

Jesus as the new humanity went to the same testing ground as his and our ancestors. As Maximus the Confessor argued, the wicked powers—seeing the Lord Jesus in human flesh as were Adam and Eve—believed him to be vulnerable to the same deceptions as the primeval couple. Jesus "submitted to it so that, by experiencing our temptations, he might provoke the evil power and thwart its attack, putting to death the very power that expected to seduce him just as it had Adam in the beginning."[4] As he stood where Adam stood, he reclaimed what Adam lost. The first Adam was tested in the God-blessed garden and fell. The second Adam was tested in the God-cursed desert, and won.

The fact that Jesus is in the desert forty days is not acci-dental. Jesus is, after all, not only reliving the universal human story—he is reliving the particular Israelite story. After Israel was "baptized" in the Red Sea, they too were led by the Spirit out into the wilderness to be tested. God was not doing evil to them there. He was instead carrying them through the wilder-ness, "as a man carries his son" (Deut. 1:31). Almost immediately the Israelites start asking themselves, "Are we really the sons of God?" They are tested there, and they turn and test God by the criteria of their desires for provision, protection, and exaltation. After enduring plagues of the same sort that fell on their enemies in Egypt, Israel refuses to be disciplined, refuses to conform to the will of God to do good to them. And so the vast majority of them are left in the wilderness, cut off from the land of promise (1 Cor. 10:5). Not even Moses—the meekest man who had ever lived—was meek enough to inherit the land (Deut. 3:23–29).

Of the entire exodus generation, only Caleb and Joshua, who had believed God's promise from the beginning and remained true to his Word, were allowed to enter the land of inheritance. Joshua led into the land the "little ones" (Deut. 1:39), those who hadn't yet been old enough to know good from evil when their parents rebelled.

Israel was never a matter of mere marking in the flesh. Those corpses in the desert all had been circumcised. The issue is instead a circumcised heart—whether one's desires conform to the desires of God (Deut. 10:16; Rom. 2:29). Jesus was tested, tested in his heart in the desert by the same tests that had felled his fathers, as to whether he is the true Israel of God, that holy nation that walks in the way of the Lord. He, as the true Joshua, is the pioneer who goes ahead of the people, scoping out the opposition ahead of time, and leading the troops when the time has arrived. Jesus was tested to see if he was Israel in his heart, if he was the Son of God.

Jesus in the wilderness was also being tested in terms of whether he was qualified to be king. The kings of Israel had, time and time again, torn down their own administrations by following after wayward desires, whether for military might, sexual pleasure, murderous vengeance, material wealth, or whatever. Jesus proved himself to meet the divine standards of Deuteronomy 17 to be monarch of the nation of Israel, to stand over his people as shepherd and as son of God.

Like the kings before him, his anointing led immediately to war. Both Saul and David after the Spirit rushed upon them were led out to wild places to fight the enemies of the people. These initial skirmishes were designed to teach them where their royal strength came from: "Not by might, nor by power, but by my Spirit, says the LORD of hosts" (Zech. 4:6).

Jesus was not only anointed to be king, but he was anointed, more specifically, to be king in the line of David. After David's anointing, David was sent away, out into the wilderness, where he was tracked down by Saul, the king who was deposed by God but who didn't yet see his reign collapsed around him. David, protected by God and gifted with wisdom, escaped Saul's snares and traps. He survived to take the throne without becoming like his enemy in the process. God promised there would be another king, an anointed one, of whom God said, "The enemy shall not outwit him; the wicked shall not humble him" (Ps. 89:22). And here he was, in the wilderness, the demon wrestler who would be king.

In any discussion of Jesus' temptations, someone will typically ask, "Could Jesus have sinned?" To answer that, I would simply say that it depends on what you mean by "could." I'll respond with another question. Think of the person you love the most. While you have this loved one's face before your mind, let me ask you: "Could you murder that person?" Your response would probably be, "Of course not!" You would then tell me how much you love the person, what the person means to you, and so forth. You're incapable of murdering this person because the very act is opposed to everything that you're about. (Note: If you answered with a cheery, "Boy, could I!" to that question, please put down this book and seek professional help.)

In your response to my question, you would be assuming "could" to mean a moral capability. But "could" here could also mean a natural ability. You tell me you "couldn't" murder your loved one, but that's no sign that you are saying you couldn't physically take this person on. You're saying you would never do such a thing.

Jesus is himself the union of God and man, with both a human and a divine nature. God is, of course, morally incapable of sinning. But Jesus, in his human nature, really desires those things humanity's been designed to desire. Could he have sinned—is his nature one that is capable of being both light and darkness? No. Could he have sinned—was he physically capable of eating bread, of throwing himself from a temple, of bowing his knee and verbalizing the words "Satan is lord"? Yes, of course.

It's at this point that we often further misunderstand Jesus' solidarity with us. We too often assume our current sinful status is what it means to be "real." That's because we've never known a world in which there is no sin. If you grow up all your life on a coastline near an uncapped oil spill, you might conclude that seagulls are covered in tar. As you read or travel, though, and see the birds in their natural state, you'll discover your experience was abnormal; that's not the way it's meant to be. Too often we dismiss as "all too human" what is not human at all; it's a satanic nature parasitically imposed on the human after the fall of Eden.

Jesus "sympathizes" with us in our temptations, the Bible tells us (Heb. 4:15). Yet we err when we think of this sympathy as some kind of psychologically motivated dismissal or minimizing of sin. Just think about the reactions if you were to sit around with your friends as you all talk about your temptations. One friend might confess to lust, and many in the group would nod heads in understanding. Another might confess an unforgiving spirit or a tendency toward hotheadedness. Again several would offer the words "I know how that is" as a means of encouragement. Probably, though, if someone were to say, "I have this persistent desire to throw kittens in a wood chipper," the nods and affirmations would end. You'd probably be nudging the person next to you under the table in disbelief and exchanging looks with the person across from you that would mean something along the lines of, "Man, is this a sick one or what!" We often are most able to justify the sins in others if they correspond with our own failings, because we understand them.[5]

Jesus, the book of Hebrews tells us, "had to be made like his brothers in every respect" (2:17). This was an act of spiritual warfare: "Since therefore the children share in flesh and blood, he himself likewise partook of the same things, that through death he might destroy the one who has the power of death, that is, the devil" (Heb. 2:14). Jesus' solidarity with us as a human being—as a "son of God"—meant that he took on everything, from sweating pores to moving bowels to firing adrenal glands.

And this humanity wasn't simply physical—"flesh" in Scripture never refers merely to the material. He also took on a human emotional, volitional, intellectual, and spiritual life. As a man, Jesus truly wanted. He could be lonely. He could be hungry. He could be angry. He could be exhausted. He experienced all of this as we do, except without sin.

We expect Jesus to have endured temptation as we endure temptation—and he did. But much of what we include in "temptation" isn't temptation at all. It's beyond our good, created desires being appealed to. It's instead those embryonic stages of sinful desire. Jesus' desert testing was indeed forty days of torture, but his torture was not because he, like we, longed to do the forbidden. It is because embedded with those good, natural human desires, he longed for what was good in each of the things he was (temporarily) denied.

The sympathy Jesus has for us isn't chiefly psychological (although our Christ does, of course, know our frame as dust and has experienced it firsthand). The sympathy here is chiefly identification. He suffered when tempted, the Bible says, and so he is "able to help those who are being tempted" (Heb. 2:18). The sympathy is about his being qualified to be "a merciful and faithful high priest" (Heb. 2:14–17)—a human mediator before God. It is then quite literally sympathy—a feeling alongside of, a compassion, a passion along with.

It was important for Jesus to assume human nature in all its aspects—including desire—because Jesus was here to transform human nature, to restore us back to the glory of the full radiance of the image of God. Just as Adam had been the alpha point of the old humanity, Jesus was to "sum up" in himself everything it means to be the new humanity before God (Eph. 1:10).

He had, therefore, to reclaim human desire under the direction of the Holy Spirit. "Although he was a son," the Bible says, "he learned obedience through what he suffered," so that "being made perfect" he could be "the source of eternal salvation to all who obey him" (Heb. 5:8–9). Jesus' sympathy for us in temptation is that in himself he sublimated the human passions ("the flesh") to the direction of God's kingdom ("the Spirit"). He transformed the human will by subduing it, through unbroken communion with his Father, to "Not my will but yours be done."[6]

This was not for himself. He had, after all, experienced this perfectly synchronized will in communion with his Father "before the world existed" (John 17:5). "And for their sakes I sanctify Myself," Jesus said of his followers, present and future, "that they also may be sanctified by the truth" (John 17:19 NKJV). Now, the same Spirit who led Jesus through this track of desert—and who raised him from the dead—flows through everyone who is attached to Jesus by faith (Romans 8), just as the nutrients flow from a vine to its branches (John 15).

As we'll see, the satanic power continually challenged Jesus at the point of what he wanted. Satan didn't propose that Jesus use his power independently, as we commonly assume. Instead he called on Jesus to direct God to use God's power for the sake of Jesus. That is, Satan wanted this son of the Father to make his desires paramount, and his communion with God a means to that end. This would unhinge, permanently, the desires of man from the good pleasure of God, keeping humanity driven along by the demonic prince through the "passions of our flesh, carrying out the desires of the body and the mind" (Eph. 2:3).

Desire is a powerful thing. Here's where Darwinism is precisely right. Whatever you may think of evolutionary thought, it really is true, isn't it, that almost no one thinks of a potential romantic interest, "There's a fine set of genetic material that could propagate my DNA successfully into the next generation." Even if that's what's behind it all (and I'd argue it's not, or at least not all that's behind it), very few of us think, "Her hips sure are wide enough for childbearing!" or "With muscles like that, he'd be able to adequately defend my offspring from predators" or whatever. We don't rationally think about why we like the foods we like either, or why we're drawn to sleeping in all morning, in one person's case, or to working compulsively, in another's. We are simply attracted toward something or someone we like, and we may not even cognitively know all the reasons why. We just want what we want, and sometimes we want what we don't want to want. There are other shepherds than just the good shepherd, and he's not the only one who leaves behind the ninety-nine to go after the one.

In the end you find yourself walking "according to the flesh"—that is, according to the creaturely aspect of yourself apart from the rule of God—rather than "according to the Spirit"—that is, according to the direction of God (Rom. 8:4–8). Whatever the desire—for food, for attention, for admiration, for adventure, for fame, for security, for whatever it is that you crave at the moment—once it's redirected away from its intended end, it becomes a master.

The pull of the passions always promises a resolution of the "burning." *I will manipulate my coworker with a morsel of office gossip, just once. I will view the pornographic image, just to see what it's like.* But the passions are a lure. Unless they find resolution in the way God designed the universe by his wisdom, they are perpetually unsatisfied.

Ultimately, then, the desires—always in search of fulfillment, never finding it—gain mastery over you (2 Pet. 2:19). Your passions, James warned the churches, "are at war within you" because you "desire and do not have," you "covet and cannot obtain" (James 4:1–2). There is no upper limit of fame that can ever satisfy those who crave it. There is no monetary figure at which those who long for financial success will ever be willing to say, "That's enough." There is no orgasm that feels good enough to last you a lifetime. As temptation moves onward and inward, you become "insatiable for sin" (2 Pet. 2:14). You're caught.

As you move along toward temptation, the demonic powers want to work in concert with, not in opposition to, what it is that you want. There's a reason, remember, why the slaughterhouse workers want to keep the cows fed and contented and unalarmed. There's a blood room at the end of the path. The lure of desire never shows up with suddenness. That would scare you away. The desires have to be cultivated little by little, until you are ready to give in to them. Esau wouldn't have contemplated an exchange as insane as an inheritance for soup if his stomach had been full. David, right after his victory over Goliath, probably would have blushed and walked away had he seen the naked Bathsheba. The fall, in every case, was a long time coming.

Temptation is, by definition, subtle and personality specific, with a strategy to enter as larvae and then emerge in the fullness of time as a destructive animal force. This is why James uses embryonic language to speak of the "lure" of desire: "Then desire when it has conceived gives birth to sin, and sin when it is fully grown brings forth death" (James 1:14–15).

You are being watched. The demonic powers have had millennia to observe human nature. But that's not enough. As the farmer-poet Wendell Berry notes of livestock husbandry, a competent farmer must know not just the nature of species and breeds of animals but also "the animal's individuality."[7] The spiritual powers out there are expert cosmic farmer-ranchers and are customizing a temptation plan that fits with the way your desires, particularly, work. They notice what turns your head, what quickens your pulse. Like the Roman guard feeling around, with a spike in one hand, on the Lord Jesus' arm, seeking his vein under the skin, the demonic beings are marking out your weak points, sizing you up so that they might crucify you. They'll find what you want, and they'll give it to you.

The foolish son in Proverbs 7 received step-by-step what he wanted. Everything, from the adulteress's desire for him to her husband's coincidental out-of-town journey, all fell into place. It must have felt like serendipity.

Sometimes Christians make decisions based on seeing opportunities come open. In our spiritual lingo we often talk about "open doors" and "closed doors" and "seeing where God is at work" in circumstances, as evidence of God's leading us to do something or other. There's a sense in which that's wisdom, observing the situation around us in order to make a decision. But sometimes people will assume the "open doors" in their lives are all signals to go forward. How could it not be right when everything just seems to be fitting together perfectly? But what if something wicked is just ahead of you, opening those doors for you, right down to the chambers of hell?

So, again, what does the testing of Jesus' desire have to do with whatever you're going through right now? Well, stop reading this for a moment and take the desert island test. Years ago a friend was telling me he feared he was unrepentant over a temptation he'd seemingly overcome years before. "I'm afraid all I've done is put myself out of the way of opportunity," he told me. He said he knew that was the case because if he were alone with what was tempting him, alone on a desert island, with no one around and no way that anyone would ever find out, "I'd just do it. I know I would."

Ask yourself that question now. Imagine you could do anything, you could make it happen exactly as you wish, and could then go back and reverse time so that it had never happened—no consequences for your life, your work, your family, or Judgment Day. What would it be? Whatever comes to mind might be a pretty good insight into where it is your desires are being farmed.

Jesus endured the desert island test. He was indeed in a deserted place, with no one around, and no one—no one of flesh and blood anyway—would ever know if he'd yielded to temptation. But he stood there, trusting and obeying, for himself and for you. Tempted and found obedient to God in his desires, Jesus is an able High Priest and head of a new humanity. He is able, through the Spirit, to conform our desires to his own, being other directed toward God and neighbor. In the meantime, there are voices all around you asking, "What do you want?"

Where Are You Going?

The slaughterhouse consultant I had heard in the interview sometimes gives tours of the plants she inspects, teaching people about how they get their meat. These can go terribly awry, she says. One woman on a tour accidentally walked, right at the start, into the blood room where the slaughters happen. Seeing the carnage everywhere, she was nauseated and traumatized. The scientist helped her calm down by taking her to an overhead catwalk where she could observe the quiet calm scene of the cattle walking quietly toward their end. With her mind off the blood she'd seen, the slaughterhouse tourist came down off the catwalk and said, "Not so bad now."[8] Seeing the final stage in isolation from the lead-up to it was a horror. Imagine how it would seem to the livestock themselves, if they could be conscious of it.

The final stage in the cycle of temptation is the challenging of your future. Desire gives way to sin, James warned, and "sin when it is fully grown brings forth death" (James 1:15). Temptation only works if the possible futures open to you are concealed. Consequences, including those of Judgment Day, must be hidden from view or outright denied.

The first temptation we see in Scripture is a contest of visions of the future. God had given humanity a picture of blessing (a fruitful universe under the rule of humanity) and a picture of curse (a universe under the reign of death). God said to the man and the woman, "Of the tree of the knowledge of good and evil you shall not eat, for in the day that you eat of it you shall surely die" (Gen. 2:17). Just as God created the humans with a drive for food, for worship, for communion, for sex, for vocation, and so forth, he also created them with a drive for life. A suicidal grasping of spiritually poisoned food isn't natural at all. In order to herd Eve along to that point, the serpent needed to offer his own vision of the future: "You will not surely die" (Gen. 3:4). He offered Eve another possible future reality: godhood apart from submission to the Creator.

But the serpent did not wish to conceal judgment from Eve permanently, but only until she could fall and lead her husband to do the same. Ultimately, after all, the serpent wasn't concerned with the tree of the knowledge of good and evil. He was concerned with the tree of life, the source of the man's and the woman's continued existence from God. The dragon knew that if they became like him, they would be separated from communion with God and in judgment would be exiled from God's sanctuary, from the presence of that life-giving tree.

Now the powers stand over humanity as accusers, the Bible reveals, indicting the race "day and night before our God" (Rev. 12:10). Why do they accuse? It's because they want the image out of the way and charged with a capital offense against the holiness of God. The powers could not ascend to the rightful throne of God, but they could ascend to the rightful throne of man. They were murderers from the beginning (John 8:44), and as far back into history as we can smell now reeks of rotting corpses and spattered blood.

In Israel's primal temptation, the future was likewise shielded from view. As is always, ultimately, the case, the desires were joined with a fear of death. When the trickster brother Jacob offered to negotiate a trade—the bowl of red stuff for the birthright (that is, Esau's claim to the firstborn's right to his father's inheritance), Esau replied with words that ought to cause us to look at the floor with shame: "I am about to die; of what use is a birthright to me?" (Gen. 25:32). But death was in that bowl.

What Esau lost was not simply his. It belonged to his entire family line, all the offspring after him. Based on his place in the order, he was to be one of the patriarchs of the people of promise, the children of "Abraham, Isaac, and Esau." But his momentary appetite derailed himself and his children, to a thousand generations. This would eventually dawn on Esau—long after he had forgotten those momentary stomach pangs and that momentary salivation for food. Yet he "found no chance to repent, though he sought it with tears" (Heb. 12:17).

Here is perhaps the most critical part of Jesus' testing in the wilderness for us. Some of Jesus' temptations seem, if we're honest, kind of trivial to us, as we'll see later. But if Jesus had succumbed to Satan's offers at any one point, he would have been a sinner. He would have been a Devil-fearer rather than a

God-fearer. He would have been disqualified from being king over Israel and king over the universe. And you and I would be in hell right now.

Jesus went out, remember, into "the wilderness." In the biblical world, the desert was dangerous at the most primal level—dry, fruitless, lonely, untamed. In a passage many ancient Christians believed spoke of the fall of Satan, the Bible speaks of the enemy as one who "shook kingdoms" and "made the world like a desert" (Isa. 14:16–17). God's judgment means a return to the earth's prehistoric state ("without form and void," Gen. 1:2), and seeing the end of God's wrath means beholding how "the fruitful land was a desert, and all its cities were laid in ruins" (Jer. 4:26). The desert images a place of literal desertion as "a lair of jackals" (Jer. 10:22). God's curse on the ground—"thorns and thistles" (Gen. 3:18)—is seen in its full force in the desert places, where, as we'll see, it is virtually impossible for man to bring forth bread from the ground (Gen. 3:17–19).

The kingdom of God that the ancient prophesies announced is the opposite of a desert; it is "like streams of water in a dry place" (Isa. 32:2), like life-giving water turning the desert into a place of trees and freshwater squirming with fish (Ezek. 47:1–12). At the end of the age, "The wilderness and the dry land shall be glad; the desert shall rejoice and blossom like the crocus" (Isa. 35:1) as "waters break forth in the wilderness, and streams in the desert" (Isa. 35:6). The people, in the end, will say, "This land that was desolate has become like the garden of Eden, and the waste and desolate and ruined cities are now fortified and inhabited" (Ezek. 36:35). When the Spirit is poured out, "the wilderness becomes a fruitful field, and the fruitful field is deemed a forest" because "justice will dwell in the wilderness" (Isa. 32:15–16). The desert into which Jesus walked was hardly fruitful, hardly glad.

The wilderness in Scripture represents not only a place of testing but also a place of judgment. Jesus as the new Adam experienced in the desert the curse brought about by the first Adam. Jesus as the new Israel labored for forty days under the wandering imposed on the old Israel for their idolatry and grumbling against God. Jesus as the new king wandered in a wasteland of exile, with no people there over whom to reign.

When our ancestors surrendered their dominion to the serpent, God announced it would not always remain so. The snake-god would be toppled, and he would be toppled through the very thing the powers hated: God's rule over the universe through an image-bearing sign, humanity. It would be, God said, "the offspring" of the woman who would pin down the serpent's head (Gen. 3:15).

In every generation, though, the serpent would sniff out the new children of man and find them all covered with the stink of death. The genealogies of the Bible—and of every other history—bear out the same end result: ". . . and he died . . . and he died . . . and he died . . . " Every death was an exposure; the corpse was seen to be part of the satanic conspiracy and was therefore cut off from the tree of life. The powers must have, for thousands of years, reassured themselves, "We shall not surely die." But now here he was, the Son of God.

Israel underwent a baptism of water in the Red Sea, but they underwent a baptism of fire in the desert. They brought upon themselves God's judgment, and the desert—intended to be a place of temporary passage, a "valley of the shadow of death" (Ps. 23:4)—instead became the execution ground of their condemnation. They thought the enemy was behind them, drowned in the sea. But the enemy behind the enemy still lurked in the desert and in their own uncircumcised hearts. Because of their constant rebellion against God, the bodies of many of them were cast down out there in the desert. To be brought through the wilderness is mercy (Ezek. 20:17). To be left in the wilderness is judgment.

John's Jewish readers knew their Bibles. They understood the concept of an animal "bearing away" human sin to the desert places. The people of Israel had been told during their desert wanderings to kill animals, the blood being shed as a sacrifice for their sins against God and presented to him by the priests.

But the priest also would lay hands on a live goat "and confess over it all the iniquities of the people of Israel, and all their transgressions, all their sins" (Lev. 16:21). After this, the priest was to lay the sins "on the head of the goat and send it away into the wilderness" (Lev. 16:21). God pronounced through Moses, "The goat shall bear all their iniquities on itself to a remote area, and he shall let the goat go free in the wilderness" (Lev. 16:22). This goat, God said, was to be presented alive and then "sent away into the wilderness to Azazel" (Lev. 16:10). Azazel is a mysterious figure in the Old Testament but is thought to be a goat demon, a feared wicked presence out there in the chaos beyond.

Sometimes Christians have debated whether we are saved from the Devil or from the wrath of God. Clearly, in Scripture the answer is both. It is God's judgment that comes against rebellious humanity. The wages of sin equals death. But being handed over to Satan is a terrifying judgment of God (1 Cor. 5:1–5). God enacts the penalty of death by handing the unrighteous over to the one who has the power of death, the Devil (Heb. 2:14). That's why one of the most terrifying judgments God laid on the Israelites in the wilderness was that of snakes.

In one of the episodes of Israelite insurrection against God in the desert, God "sent fiery serpents among the people . . . so that many people of Israel died" (Num. 21:6). When some of the people cried out for mercy, God directed Moses to make a bronze image of a snake and hoist it on a pole. "Everyone who is bitten, when he sees it, shall live," God told the people (Num. 21:8). In order to be free of the curse that had come upon them—the curse of poisonous predators and of death itself—the people had to gaze on the curse itself, high and lifted up. Jesus said this means of escape from judgment pointed to something else, something future. "And as Moses lifted up the serpent in the wilderness, so must the Son of Man be lifted up," Jesus told a visiting rabbi, "that whoever believes in him may have eternal life" (John 3:14–15).

Jesus, as the God-appointed redeemer of the world, bears our iniquities upon himself (Isa. 53:4–5). He becomes a curse for us, by bearing the penalty of the law (Gal. 3:13). His identification with that curse doesn't start as the nails of Golgotha are driven into his hands. The identification of Jesus with our judgment starts in his baptism of repentance—for us—and as he goes for the first time "outside the camp" (Heb. 13:13) for us to meet the holder of our ancient curse.

Jesus in the wilderness is preparing himself for sacrifice as both the one who is offering and as the offering itself. As the offering, he is tested and found to be without spot, without blemish. As the High Priest, he is found to be worthy of entering the presence of God to offer blood that is his own. Like every high priest, though, he must be one of the people he represents ("chosen from among men . . . to act on behalf of men in relation to God"), and he must be chosen by God ("no one takes this honor for himself") (Heb. 5:1, 4).

Even as distant as we are from the ancient Hebrews, we can understand something of the justice of this. Suppose you were on trial for a crime. Theoretically, I suppose, a computer program could compare the laws of your state to the entered data about the facts of your case. You probably wouldn't want that. You'd want a jury of fellow human beings, your peers. Now imagine the same courtroom, but this time you're there not as a defendant but as a grieving family member testifying against the serial killer who took the life of someone close to you. Would it matter to you if the judge were himself a serial killer? Of course it would. It would be unjust, and you'd protest as much as you could.

"Therefore he had to be made like his brothers in every respect, so that he might become a merciful and faithful high priest in the service of God, to make propitiation for the sins of the people," the Scripture says. "For because he himself has suffered when tempted, he is able to help those who are being tempted" (Heb. 2:17–18). He is able to offer the sacrifice because he is one of us, tested to the core, "yet without sin" (Heb. 4:15).

Here in the desert what is foreshadowed is the cross and the resurrection to come. The presence of the Spirit before and after the temptation narratives cannot be overemphasized (Luke 4:1, 14). The Spirit, after all, is the sign of anointing, of God's presence with his king. When Saul rebelled against God, the Spirit was taken from him, a fate David pleaded against in his repentance after his episode of predatory sex and murder (Ps. 51:11). Jesus was tempted and tried and still came back with the same Spirit resting on him who had come upon him in the water and had led him into the desert. He endured suffering, but he was not abandoned to the grave.

Even in the desert, God was so present with Jesus that we see a picture before our eyes not just of God's future judgment but also of God's future peace on the other side. "And he was with the wild animals, and the angels were ministering to him" (Mark 1:13). Unlike his ancestors, Adam and Israel, Jesus is not prey for the predatory beasts. They recognize his kingship. He is not held back from paradise by a fiery angelic sword. They recognize that, too. He demonstrates in himself the restored peace between the human and angelic and animal orders that the Scripture prophesies for the day in which sin is wiped away and death is no more (Isa. 9:1–7). The kingdom of God is among humans now, just as the voice crying in the wilderness said.

As you and I trek through the wilderness, the tempting powers will attempt, as they did with our ancestors and with Jesus, to distort the way we see our future. It doesn't matter if I know that eating deep-fat-fried doughnuts every morning can raise my cholesterol levels, unless I also can imagine the possibility of a heart attack. I choose to give my children building blocks and not matches to play with because I can imagine what it would be like to see my house burning down. As a church member tells me that the one gray hair on the top of my head is "distracting" to him, I choose to listen patiently rather than to put him in a headlock and wrestle him to the floor. That's because I can foresee what it would be like to lose my opportunity to serve Christ in ministry (and, of course, because it would be wrong). A loss of future perspective makes you crazy.

Almost every adultery situation I've ever seen, for instance, includes a cheating spouse who honestly believes that he or she is not going to get caught. The cheater often doesn't want the marriage to end in divorce but instead wants to keep everything the same—spouse, kids, and lover, too. That's irrational and completely contrary to the way the world works. But you can convince yourself—or be convinced—that it will work for you. You're special, after all. That's the way temptation functions. We put consequences out of our minds, both temporal and eternal consequences.

When it comes to God, we convince ourselves that God doesn't see (Ps. 10:11; 94:7) or that he'll never call us to account (Ps. 10:13), but in order to do that we have to quiet our God-designed conscience that points continually to the criteria by which we'll be judged before the Creator's tribunal (Rom. 2:16).

The demonic powers not only will give us what we crave, but they will assist us in covering it over, for a little while. That's precisely the irony. Often you are fueled on from one temptation to the other because you haven't been caught. This gives you an illusion of a cocoon protecting you from justice. The powers, though, don't want you to get caught—not yet, not this early in the march to the slaughterhouse. They don't have a mere seventy or eighty years to live. They are ancient and patient and quite willing to wait until your downfall will bring with it the most catastrophic consequences—for you, for your family, for the kingdom of God, and to the image of Christ you carry. So they'll help you cover it all up, and then they'll expose you—mercilessly. You'll never see it coming around the bend.

Where before the invisible presences disputed the contents of the law, now they remind us of it in every jot and tittle, and how we've violated it. Where before they'd scoffed with us even of the possibility of future judgment, now they wish to hold its certainty ever before our eyes. They accuse us with our own transcribed consciences as evidence. And we know they're right.

That's what makes Jesus' wilderness temptations so liberating for us. Yes, he was being assaulted by the demonic powers.

They sought to accuse him. But he was also being tried and tested by his Father, a visible demonstration of his integrity of heart. It is through the Spirit of this Christ that David sang out to God, "You have tried my heart, you have visited me by night, you have tested me, and you will find nothing" (Ps. 17:3).

Unlike Adam and Israel and me, Jesus always remembered his future. In the face of satanic temptation, he didn't buckle because he had nothing to hide. As Jesus said on his way to the Place of the Skull, "The ruler of this world is coming. He has no claim on me" (John 14:30). The kingdom comes through a tempted, tested, triumphant Christ. In the meantime, the old desert demon still asks us, "Where are you going?"

CONCLUSION

You are on the verge of wrecking your life. I know that with certainty. I'm not psychic, and I'm not reading your mind as you read this chapter. I doubt this book will be in print long enough to be read by artificially intelligent androids; so for now, I'm assuming if you can read, I know you're human. And if you're human you've been designed to picture God—more specifically to picture the union of God and humanity in the man named Jesus.

This means, if the ancient Scriptures are right (and I'm wagering my life, and the next one, that they are), unseen spiritual beings out there are disturbed by what you are reminding them of. By the "you" in the last sentence, I don't mean a generic colloquial use of "one" or "humanity" in general. I mean *you* personally and specifically.

You may not be a Christian or even particularly religious, but if you're human, some cosmic rulers see in you the threat of an ancient oracle—that one day someone like you, a human born of a woman, would crush their skulls (Gen. 3:15). You may never have thought of yourself as similar to Jesus. But you are more like him than you know, or maybe even than you want to be.

The cosmic story of horror interrupts your personal story, and it's dangerous if you can't see where. But between Eden and you, there's a Judean wilderness. That's where Jesus stood down every test, every strategy you'll ever encounter—and he won. That's why, though we are "regarded as sheep to be slaughtered" (Rom. 8:36), "we are more than conquerors through him who loved us" (Rom. 8:37).

But in order to conquer, you must face reality. Don't mistake the stillness of your conscience for freedom from temptation. The Scripture says that temptation is "common to man" (1 Cor. 10:13). The issue isn't whether you're tempted, but whether you're aware of it and striking back. You are on the verge of wrecking your life. We all are.

Forces are afoot right now, negotiating how to get you fat enough for consumption and how to get you calmly and without struggle to the cosmic slaughterhouse floor. The easiest life for you will be one in which you don't question these things, a life in which you simply do what seems natural. The ease of it all will seem to be further confirmation that this is the way things ought to be. It might even seem as though everything is happening exactly as you always hoped it would. You might feel as though your life situation is like progressing up a stairway so perfect it's as though it was designed just for you. And it is.

In many ways the more tranquil you feel, the more endangered you are. As you find yourself curving around the soft corners of your life, maybe you should question the quietness of it all. Perhaps you should listen, beneath your feet, for the gentle clatter of hooves.

3

STARVING TO DEATH

Why We'd Rather Be Fed Than Fathered

There's nothing quite as bleak as a city street the morning after Mardi Gras. The steam of the morning humidity rises silently over asphalt, riddled with forgotten doubloons, broken bottles, littered cigarettes, used condoms, clotted blood, and mangled vomit. This sight was, where I grew up in my coastal Mississippi town, a parable for the more committed evangelicals about what was wrong with a culturally accommodated Christianity. I wasn't so sure.

My quirky little strip of home, Biloxi, was an outpost of a Catholic majority situated right at the bottom of the Bible belt of the old Confederacy. We were more New Orleans than Tupelo, and I lived in both worlds. Half my family was Southern Baptist and the other half Roman Catholic. I could see the best sides of either and the dark sides of both. I saw Catholic casino night fund-raisers and Baptist business meetings, and neither seemed to look much like the book of Acts. When it came to the ecclesial divide between Catholics and evangelicals, I was sure there must be some big differences that resulted in something as historic as the Protestant Reformation, but day to day those differences seemed to my friends and me to amount to little more than who had a black spot on their foreheads once a year and whose parents drank beer right out in the open. For the grown-ups, though, at least for the grown-ups outside my mixed-together family, these differences seemed to matter a lot. Much of that was summed up in Mardi Gras.

I loved (and love) Mardi Gras. I suppose that's because all I saw were the traditions and rituals—king cakes and parades and candy—rather than the full Bourbon Street experience. Drunkenness and immorality are indefensible, of course, but at its most innocent level, Mardi Gras replays something of God's provision for the prophet Elijah who, like Jesus, went out into the wilderness to fast for forty days. Before he went, the angels gave him "a cake baked on hot stones." After his feast, the prophet "went in the strength of that food forty days and forty nights" (1 Kings 19:6–8).

But some of the older Baptists at my church downright hated the whole idea of Fat Tuesday. They knew that Mardi Gras was the day before the beginning of Lent, the forty days of fasting rooted, in part, in Jesus' time without food in the wilderness temptations, and they saw this party as blasphemy. "Those Catholics—they just go out and get as drunk as they want to, eat till they vomit," I remember one neo-Puritan naysayer lamenting. "They're just getting it all out of their system before they have to get all somber and holy for Lent." It never made an anti-Catholic out of me because I never saw any of my devout Catholic relatives or friends behaving that way. But it made sense to me that gorging and getting drunk the day before Ash Wednesday probably wasn't what the Lord meant when he said to "repent, for the kingdom of God is at hand."

As the years have gone by, though, I'm realizing that we Baptists had a Mardi Gras, too. Mardi Gras Protestantism didn't celebrate the day just on a yearly calendar, though, but, much more importantly, on the calendar of a lifespan. The typical cycle went something like this. You were born, then reared up in Sunday school until you were old enough to raise your hand when the teacher asked who believes in Jesus and wants to go to heaven. At that point you were baptized, usually long before the first pimple of puberty, and shortly thereafter you had your first spaghetti dinner fund-raiser to go to summer youth camp.

And then sometime between fifteen and twenty you'd go completely wild.

Our view of the "College and Career" Sunday school class was somewhat like our view of purgatory. It might be there, technically, but there was no one in it. After a few years of carnality, you'd settle down, start having kids, and you'd be back in church, just in time to get those kids into Sunday school and start the cycle all over again. If you didn't get divorced or indicted, you'd be chairman of deacons or head of the women's missionary auxiliary by the time your own kids were going completely wild. It was just kind of expected. You were going to get things out of your system before you settled down. You know, I never could find that in the book of Acts either.

I never really went through the wild stage. But years later, having lived a fairly upstanding life externally, I found myself envying a Christian leader giving his "testimony." This man described his life of mind-blowing drugs, manic sex, and non-stop partying in such detail that, before I knew it, I was wistfully thinking, *Wouldn't that be the best of both worlds? All that, and heaven, too.* I'd embraced the dark side of Mardi Gras in my own mind. As much as I thought I was superior to both the drunken partiers on the streets and the dour cranks condemning it, I had internalized the hidden hedonism of it all. I was under the lordship of Christ but, if only for that moment, wishing for the lordship of my own fallen appetite.

The first temptation of Christ is all about this. When Jesus walked out from his baptism into the desert, the Bible tells us he was tracked down by the Devil, the old serpent of Eden. And, just as in Eden, Satan offered Jesus food. "If you are the Son of God," the Devil said, "command these stones to become loaves of bread" (Matt. 4:3). What Satan prompted Jesus to do was to provide for himself, to feed himself, or, rather, to use the power of the Spirit to feed himself. It was the pull to consumption, to self-provision.

When offered the chance to satisfy his hunger, Jesus repeated to the Devil an ancient passage of Scripture: "Man shall not live by bread alone, but by every word that comes from the mouth of God" (Matt. 4:4). Often Christians see this as just a reminder that, like Jesus, we ought to have Bible verses memorized, ready to deploy in a time of temptation. There's certainly some truth to that. Jesus probably learned this verse from his carpenter father or with the other Nazarene Jewish children at the synagogue from the tribal elders there. It was bound up in his heart, just as Moses had commanded. But there was more to it than that. Jesus' response showed he recognized what was happening around him, that he was repeating another story. He was saying to this dark power before him, "I know who you are, and I know what you're doing. And I know who I am, and I know what I'm doing."

It is no accident that our ancient foe first appears in Holy Scripture as a snake—imagery that follows the Devil all the way through the canon of Scripture to the closing vision of the Revelation of John. As philosopher Leon Kass puts it, "For the serpent is a mobile digestive tract that swallows its prey whole; in this sense the serpent stands for pure appetite."[1] Indeed he does—and the whole of Scripture and of Christian tradition warns the church against the way of the appetites, the way of consuming oneself to death.

We are commanded away from the path of Esau, who sells his inheritance for a pile of red stew (Heb. 12:16–17). We're directed away from the god of the belly (Phil. 3:19). From the tree in the garden to the wilderness beyond the Jordan to the present hour, the people of God are tempted to turn their digestive or reproductive tracts away from the mystery of Christ and toward the self as God. Here the Spirit of the Christ and the spirit of the age are warring right now for your heart, for your soul, and for your stomach. And what we'll have to decide is whether we'd rather be fed or fathered.

A QUESTION OF APPETITE

As Jesus walked into the demon-haunted wasteland, the first thing the Scripture tells us is that he was hungry. On the one hand, most of you reading this have no idea what I'm writing about, and neither do I. Very few of us have ever been truly hungry, at least not with the kind of hunger a forty-day fast would leave behind. On the other hand, most of us can imagine something of the sensation because we've all been hungry.

Have you ever been in the flow of working on something so much that at the end of the day you realized you'd simply forgotten to eat? Did you notice yourself becoming a little lightheaded, headachy, irritable, or weak? Rarely do we ever go very long without recognizing the need for food, though. The appetite is created to prompt us toward nutrition.

God did not design human beings to eat on the basis of reason alone. The appetites are there to drive us toward what we need, whether it's food or sleep or sex or something else. God could have called together a universe where you would regularly find yourself saying things like, "My fat reserves are now alarmingly low, so I must eat food for sustenance" or "Based on my calculations, my hydration levels are below the acceptable minimum, so let's drink" or "Our marriage should be unified through sexual intercourse, and children are a blessing, so let's copulate." We can, of course, order those things out rationally, as anyone who's ever been on a weight-loss program, a diabetes regimen, or fertility treatments knows. But typically we're alerted to a need because of a bodily sign, an appetite.

The appetites are part of the desires we discussed in the last chapter, but they are more specifically bodily in nature, pointing and driving toward a need that the creature has. Typically the appetites drive us toward the sustenance of some creaturely need—food, sleep, sex, and so forth. Sometimes we create artificial appetites through habitual use of something that can be just as strong or stronger than the natural appetites. Some of you who have tried to quit smoking cigarettes know something of this, as do those of you who have stopped using some kind of addictive drug. Even in the more mundane sense, we can create an appetite for something such as caffeine or a runner's high that then becomes part of the body's ongoing expectation unless trained otherwise. The appetites are strong, and strong by design.

The hunger of Jesus was the arena of the demon's first strike. Going without food for forty days is a dangerous prospect under any circumstances, much less in an arid, isolated wilderness. A weak, dehydrated man could easily faint on the rocks and become easy prey for the wild animals prowling about. Jesus' hunger here wasn't simply a matter of discomfort; he was in genuine physical jeopardy. At this moment of weakness Satan appealed to Jesus' appetite not simply by suggesting the practical ("make something edible to satisfy your hunger") but by calling forward the visual ("turn these stones into loaves of bread"). He appealed to Jesus' appetites through the imagination.

Bread is important here. Satan, after all, could have referenced virtually anything that could have provided basic nutrients. Pureed rat meat, for instance, would be digested just as well. But when the unclean spirit mentioned "loaves of bread," he was pointing to something familiar, tapping into what psychologists call a trigger for the appetites.

Jesus was literally born and bred for bread. He first saw the light of day in Bethlehem—literally "House of Bread." And bread was a dietary staple for any Middle Eastern man of the time. Jesus probably remembered what it was like to come back from an exhausting day on the work site with his father and smell bread baking on a fire outside his parents' hut. As Satan spoke, Jesus might have even imagined it there before him, the sensation of breaking open the crust to the hot yeasty stuff inside. That is human in the most basic sense of the word.

The "loaves of bread," moreover, were contrasted with "these stones." If you are Middle Eastern or African you probably have a better feel for the setting here than do those of us from American, European, or Asian backgrounds. Some of us tend to think of "wilderness" here as a forest or woodland. Even when we come to understand that Jesus was sojourning in a desert, we still tend to see it as a vast tract of sand, like a beach with no ocean. But this place, the Judean wilderness, was a craggy field of stone. There were probably rocks as far as Jesus could see. Satan offered him a way of escape from his rocky exile.

"If you are the Son of God, command these stones to become . . . bread" (Matt. 4:3). These temptations were real, not a charade. This was not the equivalent of your saying, "I'm really tempted to levitate up from where I'm sitting right now and shoot laser beams from my hands." Through the miracle-working Spirit upon him, Jesus could really turn the stones to bread. And he really wanted the bread. This hunger didn't start forty days prior. This gnawing was hidden in human nature ever since something wicked stalked a woman way back there in our collective past. Jesus stepped into Eve's hunger and Israel's and ours.

As the son of Eve, Jesus joined her in her temptation. She, after all, was appealed to through the appetite, also through visual and imaginative as well as digestive appeals. The fruit from that tree of knowledge of good and evil was good for food, beautiful to the eyes, and able to make her wise. And she, like Jesus, had the power to grasp it. All she had to do was reach out and draw it to her mouth.

The issue was fatherhood. That was what was at the root of Satan's temptation, which is why he prefaced his offer with the questioning clause, "If you are the Son of God . . ." In order to see this, you need, partly, to step back into the ancient agrarian world of the Bible. There were no child support attorneys or state welfare offices. A man who would not feed his family was a disgrace to his tribe. This is at the root of Jesus' teaching that even the evil would not give their child a snake when he asked for a fish, or a stone if he asked for bread.

I say you must *partly* step back into the context to see this, but you need not do so fully because, intuitively, you know this too. Think of the most callous and neglectful father you know. Can you imagine that man throwing pebbles into the mouth of his toddler child as the baby pleads for something to eat? I'd guess probably not. We seem to know, from a religious or psychological or even a Darwinist vantage point, that such a scenario just isn't normal. Fatherhood isn't just about biological kinship; it's also about provision, among other things.

Those reared up with the Torah, the written law of God, understood in a veiled sense what would soon be further unveiled in the Christian gospel, that human fatherhood is modeled after the divine patriarchy (Eph. 3:14–15). This is why Jesus taught us to pray "Our Father" along with him (Matt. 6:9), because in Christ we participate mystically in the Father/Son dynamic that's at the heart of the universe (John 17:24). Human fathers are to bring forth bread for their families because that's precisely what a Father God does for his own sons and daughters.

This is where Eve fell, and Adam right behind her. Satan suggested, back in the garden, that somehow God was withholding something good from the humans, something that, in fact, would make them like him. Eve started to see God not as Father but as rival, and that's when she struck out to grab what he was holding back from her. Her appetites, Satan said, were a more reliable guide to what she needed than the word of her God.

Satan also had seen the bloated corpse of another "son of God" out there in the wilderness centuries before Jesus came. The Israelites had also eaten themselves to death. In the march out of Egypt—"baptized" by the Red Sea (1 Cor. 10:2)—the people of Israel were likewise tested to see if they recognized God as a providing Father. God provided his people with manna, a kind of bread that would appear suddenly on the ground. He showered them with quail and sent water suddenly springing from a rock at the spoken command of God's prophet. But the people soon rebelled against the voice of their God. They had a "craving" (Num. 11:4).

God created this craving in the first place. It was he, after all, who had spoken to the Israelites of their land of promise in such imaginatively sensory terms, as a land oozing with milk and honey. It was he who told them about the agricultural possibilities awaiting them, the abundant harvest to come, and the bread they would eat without fill.

But they never quite believed him. When shown the manna for the first time, Israel dismissively asked, "What is it?" (Ex. 16:15). When God delivered the supernatural bread to them, "fine as frost on the ground," (v. 14) some of them tried to hoard it, just in case God didn't come through with a fresh supply the next day. Their stored-up surplus, though, was found to be writhing with maggots (Ex. 16:14, 19–20).

The Israelites understood the connection between father-hood and bread, a connection they would make repeatedly through the years. During their exile and the destruction of their homeland, Jeremiah the prophet would weep because the lack of bread was evidence that the people of Israel had become "orphans, fatherless" (Lam. 5:3). Ezekiel used very similar lan-guage (Ezek. 4:17).

In their desert trek, Israel came to conclude that God was not a Father. They started to theorize that God had brought them into the wilderness to condemn them rather than to save them. The test revealed that the word of God was a slave to their stomachs and not the other way around as they engaged in slave nostalgia. "Would that we had died by the hand of the LORD in the land of Egypt, when we sat by the meat pots and ate bread to the full," they grumbled, "for you have brought us out into this wilderness to kill this whole assembly with hunger" (Ex. 16:3). Do you see what happened? They actually envied the floating corpses of the Egyptians they'd seen in the sea. At least those mortified corpses had full stomachs.

The test revealed they wanted a Pharaoh more than a Father. They didn't remember the tyranny, the slavery, or the peril of death back in their land of sojourn. They remembered instead what became more important to them—the demands of their appetites. "We remember the fish we ate in Egypt that cost nothing," they said, "the cucumbers, the melons, the leeks, the onions, and the garlic" (Num. 11:5). In a slap of ingratitude they said of their God, "But now our strength is dried up, and there is nothing at all but this manna to look at" (Num. 11:6). They concluded it was "better for us in Egypt" (Num. 11:18). They would rather be slaves than sons.

It wasn't just that they wished to be Egyptians; they had indeed become Egyptians in their hearts. The Egyptian religion behind them and the Canaanite religions before them—with their pantheons of fertility and sun and rain deities who existed to grow crops, conceive livestock, and feed bellies—pictured the divine as centering on filling human appetites. Jesus would identify the same tendency in his ministry when by the lake of Galilee he, too, gave supernatural bread to the crowds and then pronounced that they were seeking him "because you ate your fill of the loaves" (John 6:26). Jesus was a food-delivery system for these crowds, not a Messiah. For Israel, God had become just another Pharaoh to be cast off when he wasn't delivering the goods.

Jesus' forefather David had also hungered in the wilderness. David had sung then, "My flesh faints for you, as in a dry and weary land where there is no water" (Ps. 63:1). Even in his hunger, though, David sang also, "My soul will be satisfied as with fat and rich food" (Ps. 63:5). God fed David with exactly what he needed exactly when he needed it, and in the meantime the Spirit prompted David to see that at the end of the hunger would be "a table" (Ps. 23:5).

That's the point of the satanic suggestion to Jesus. By showing him the rocks, Satan seemed to imply, "You need bread, but all your Father says is, 'Let him eat slate.'" If Jesus had used the Spirit upon him to turn the bread into stones, he would have been rejecting his Father's promise, turning instead to his stomach at the command of Satan. He would have been, like us, enslaved to the serpent through the desires of the body and the mind. God forbid.

Jesus told the Devil that man does not live by bread alone. Notice that he didn't deny that man lives by bread. Jesus took the appetites seriously, and so did the Devil. The saliva bubbling in Jesus' mouth at the mention of bread had dribbled down the faces of his ancestors before him. And a watching demon knew. He still does.

Israel's lament, "Let's go back to Egypt, where at least we have food to eat," makes sense on the face of it. It is, if you think about it, the same feeling expressed by Esau before them: "What is my birthright to me when I am about to die?" It's the sentiment captured by the prophet Isaiah and the apostle Paul in the saying, "Let us eat and drink, for tomorrow we die" (Isa. 22:13; 1 Cor. 15:32). If all that awaits you is unconsciousness in a worm-filled tomb, then, yes, tickling every sensory node and exciting every gland and feeding every urge is probably the only alternative left.

But Jesus knew this wasn't the way the universe was crafted. There's a table on the other side of death's end, a wedding feast in fact, in which there is "a feast of rich food, a feast of well-aged wine, of rich food full of marrow, of aged wine well refined" (Isa. 25:6). Jesus knew that he would eat bread when "it is fulfilled in the kingdom of God" (Luke 22:16). Until then, the future king was willing to feast or to fast, whatever seemed best to his Father.

Moreover, Jesus knew that the path to this future blessing was through listening, not commanding. He heeded a different voice than the reptilian one in his ear at the moment and thus refused to speak the words that could have softened the stone into bread. Jesus understood that man "lives" by every word that proceeds from the mouth of God.

The way of Satan, the way of Esau, the way of lost Israel leads to a heightening of the appetite, not to a diminishing. It leads to insatiability. The end result of self-provision isn't satisfaction but instead revulsion. As novelist Frederick Buechner defines it, "Lust is the craving for salt of a person who is dying of thirst."[2]

Jesus knew that by the time Esau's red soup was digesting in his stomach, he was weeping to have that moment back, to have that birthright back. Jesus knew that the Israelites had the bread and quail they demanded, so much that they vomited it up. He would ultimately see that his follower-to-be Judas would get the money he wanted, that thirty pieces of silver, but he'd use it to buy the land where he would lie twisting over his own tangled intestines. The bread of demons, Jesus knew, leaves you dead in the end.

As this temptation wages war on us right now, the first step we need to take to break its power is to recognize what the appetites are there for in the first place. And that means recovering a sense of who you are apart from what you want. The world around you often defines you in terms of what you want. The advertising world sees you as a consumer, defined by your buying power and product preferences. Beyond that, other forces would seek to define you by your appetites themselves. If you want to drink, you're a drunk. If you want to have sex, then that's your "need" and you must "be true to yourself." And so it goes. But you don't live by bread alone. You are not what you want.

Sometimes we actually empower Satan by the way we speak of Christian conversion. We highlight the testimony of the ex-alcoholic who says, "Since I met Jesus I've never wanted another drink." Now that happens sometimes, and we should give thanks for God's power here. But this liberation is no more miraculous, indeed in some ways less so, than the testimony of the repentant drunk who says, "Every time I hear a clink of ice in a glass I tremble with desire, but God is faithful in keeping me sober."

The girl with same-sex desires might conclude she is doomed to be a lesbian because she isn't drawn to boys and still fights her attraction to girls. Family members who have to cut up their credit cards to keep from spending every paycheck on what they see advertised may conclude they're just not "spiritual" enough to follow Christ because they still war against their wants. Nonsense. You are not what you want. You are who you are. And that's defined by the Word of God. It might be that God frees your appetite from whatever it's drawn toward, but usually he instead enables you to fight it. This might go on for forty days, for forty years, for an entire lifetime. That's all right. There must be room then in our churches for a genuine bearing of one another's burdens when it comes to the appetites. Pretending the appetites are instantly nullified by conversion is a rejection of what God has told us—that we are still in the war zone.

God breaks the illusions of temptation by showing us why the appetites were created in the first place and why they're so powerful. The appetites don't exist for themselves but for a deeper spiritual reality. The Israelites of old probably thought the manna and the water were simply all about sustaining them through their trek through the desert. That's partly true. The more spiritually aware among them probably recognized that God was also teaching them something about his character, about life in his reign. And that's even more accurate. But in the fullness of time the mystery of Christ unveiled what was really at the core of God's feeding his people.

The crowds around Jesus demanded to see a sign from him, a sign that would result in filled stomachs for them. Instead of Jesus commanding stones to become bread, the crowds commanded Jesus to bring forth bread, all along citing Scripture, chapter and verse: "Our fathers ate the manna in the wilderness; as it is written, 'He gave them bread from heaven to eat'" (John 6:31). Jesus shocked the crowds, first of all, by seeming to disparage Moses. "Moses didn't give you anything," he said in essence, "but my Father gives you the true bread from heaven" (John 6:32).

Jesus further seemed to dismiss the narrative that had given shape to the entire self-identity of the nation of Israel. "Your fathers ate the manna in the wilderness, and they died," he said. "This is the bread that comes down from heaven, so that one may eat of it and not die" (John 6:49–50). Jesus then further offended the crowd by identifying himself as the true manna from God. "If anyone eats of this bread, he will live forever," he announced. "And the bread that I will give for the life of the world is my flesh" (John 6:51).

God provided his people with bread from the sky and with

water from the rock for the purpose of whetting an appetite for the gospel. He let them hunger and filled their hunger so that they would see a sign of what it means to "hunger and thirst for righteousness" (Matt. 5:6) and to have that craving filled by the gospel of Christ Jesus. Indeed, we could go back even further and wonder why God created humanity to survive by eating in the first place—nutrients from the outside assimilated into the body so that you become what you eat. God did not design the gospel after eating. He designed eating after the pattern of Christ, for whom and through whom all things were created (Col. 1:16; John 1:1; Heb. 1:2). When we learn to ask for "daily bread," we learn what it is to say "Our Father" (Matt. 6:9, 11).

This is why Jesus, when he met a woman from Samaria at Jacob's well, turned the subject from her physical thirst to her deeper need for what he called "living water" (John 4:10). Jesus assured her that the water he provided, unlike the temporal water she craved, satisfies permanently. She wondered, "Are you greater than our father Jacob?" (John 4:12). Indeed he was, and is. Jesus was no Esau, the red, grasping, hairy man of the fields. And he wasn't Jacob either—at least not the old Jacob who manipulated with words in order to steal away an inheritance. Jesus was a new Jacob—the Israel of God. He was the One who would wrestle with God in the wilderness and not let go until he blessed him. He was the One who would walk away, with a limp, yes, but who would walk away.

Don't let your urges scare you. Let them instead drive you to pray for the wisdom to see what you were created to be and to do. Watch the triggers in your life that lead you to hunger for what you want, and be warned. But in the meantime seek to direct your appetites toward the ways in which the Word of God and the order of the universe tell us they can be fulfilled. And then seek to learn to long more for their ultimate resolution in a new creation.

This is another reason why the church shouldn't neglect the Word of God, in every form God has given his Word—not just written or spoken propositions. God knows our frame, and he knows we must not only cogitate on his Word—we must chew, swallow, and digest it. The Lord's Supper is Jesus' sign in bread and wine of his presence with us, of his dawning kingdom. Every time we gather together to eat bread and drink wine together, we hear Jesus announcing, "Your sensory appetites are real and good and created, and they are pointing beyond themselves to something beyond all you could ask for or even imagine."

The Lord's Table, then, isn't just a visual aid to remind us, as though it were a memory-jogging tool. As we gather together around the Table, we are being trained to eat at the "big table" in Jerusalem. And we're announcing to ourselves, and to the satanic powers in the air around us, what's really true. "Eat, drink, and be merry, for tomorrow we die" is a sham. The alternative is not a refusal to eat, drink, or be merry. That would be ingratitude. Instead, with the resurrected Jesus we sing out, "Let us eat, drink, and be merry, for yesterday we were dead."

Jesus' words to the crowds of Galilee aren't shocking to us anymore. We hear him say, "Eat my flesh and drink my blood," and we interpret them on our church-front Communion tables. But Jesus' words would have caused the crowds to gasp and some among them to stifle vomit. Here is this suspected cult leader saying, "In order to follow me, you'll have to chew my skin and suck my blood." That is bizarre and creepy sounding in any culture, but especially in a culture where it is forbidden to even touch a human corpse or to eat any kind of bloody meat since "the life of the flesh is in the blood" (Lev. 17:11).

As we feed at the Lord's Table, of course, we are focusing our affections on the cross. "For as often as you eat this bread and drink the cup," the apostle Paul teaches us, "you proclaim the Lord's death until he comes" (1 Cor. 11:26). Of course. God's provision for our appetites is tied up completely in that Skull Place execution, which is itself tied up in those wilderness temptations.

Our salvation hinged on Jesus' mouth. Satan directed Jesus to speak, not to God but to the stones themselves, to command them to become bread. "Out of the abundance of the heart the mouth speaks" (Matt. 12:34). Israel of old had lost their inheritance by using their mouths to speak to one another rather than to God, grumbling at God's provision and discipline. Moses had lost his part in the inheritance by using his mouth to speak to the rebellious people rather than to the Rock—as God had commanded him (Num. 20:8–13).

There in the silences of the desert night, Jesus refused to use his mouth to eat. He refused to use his mouth to call forth forbidden bread. But he did open his mouth to convey remembered promises: "I will feed you with the heritage of Jacob your father, for the mouth of the LORD has spoken" (Isa. 58:14). That heritage may have been stolen at first by the trickery of a deceiver's mouth. But now the inheritance was earned by a true Son, one who didn't need to trick his Father to win a place at his table.

What Jesus learned in the wilderness that day will carry us all the way to our final redemption. Jesus was crucified for food. He absorbed "the curse of the law" of those hanged on a tree (Gal. 3:13). That curse is defined in the Law of Moses in the larger context of how to deal with a "rebellious son" who refuses to "obey the voice of his father or the voice of his mother, . . . though they discipline him" (Deut. 21:18). This rebellion is evidenced in, among other things, the rebellious son being charged as "a glutton and a drunkard" before the elders of the city (Deut. 21:20). Indeed, Jesus was charged with being "a glutton and a drunkard" (Matt. 11:19; Luke 7:34), but he wasn't.

He died, after all, thirsty. He refused to drink the wine offered him by his torturers, but he accepted the cup of God's wrath, the cup of blood soup, in our stead. Jesus knew of what the prophet Isaiah spoke: "When the poor and needy seek water, and there is none, and their tongue is parched with thirst, I the LORD will answer them; I the God of Israel will not forsake them" (Isa. 41:17). Interestingly, God said through Isaiah, "I will make the wilderness a pool of water, and the dry land springs of water" (Isa. 41:18). Jesus learned to trust this, for us, in the desert.

Jesus was willing to starve rather than eat at the table of demons, all the while convinced that his God could spread a table for him in the midst of his enemies (Ps. 23:5). In other words, Jesus heard the voice of his Father and believed the words, "You are my beloved Son; with you I am well pleased" (Luke 3:22). Those invisible words were louder for him than a stomach's growl.

A QUESTION OF DISCIPLINE

It is not by bread alone, Jesus said, that a man lives, but by every word that comes out of God's mouth. Jesus knew exactly what kind of story he'd walked into, which is why he quoted from the eighth chapter of Deuteronomy. In the text Jesus referenced here, Moses was explaining to the people of Israel the meaning of their wilderness wanderings over the past forty years. "And you shall remember the whole way that the LORD your God has led you these forty years in the wilderness," Moses said, "that he might humble you, testing you to know what was in your heart, whether you would keep his commandments or not" (Deut. 8:2).

But rebuking the Devil, Jesus showed not only that he was unwilling to question his Father's provision but also that he was unwilling to quarrel with his Father's discipline. This was at the crux of his fathers' rebellion. "They tested God in their heart by demanding the food they craved" (Ps. 78:18). Jesus knew he had been brought out here to be tested, not in order that he could test his Father.

In the Deuteronomy text, God showed his people that their time in the desert wasn't accidental, nor was it punitive. He was shaping and forming them for their time in the land of promise. "And he humbled you and let you hunger and fed you with manna, which you did not know, nor did your fathers know," Moses said, "that he might make you know that man does not live by bread alone" (Deut. 8:3).

Notice that Israel's discipline came at three points: in lack of food ("let you hunger"), in God's extraordinary provision ("fed you with manna"), but also in his ordinary provision. In the Deuteronomy text God said to the Israelites, "Your clothing did not wear out on you and your foot did not swell these forty years" (Deut. 8:4). You know, they probably never even noticed that. Probably no one brought that up as they moved from tent to tent gossiping about how awful it was to be the wilderness warriors, all by themselves. Farther back, it is clear that, as she stood before the snake, Eve wasn't aware of how God had given her every tree of the garden, every tree but one.

That's not that unusual, at least not in this fallen cosmos. How often do we notice the things that haven't happened to us? If we survive a heart attack, we might feel a sense of gratitude for being spared. We might even feel that way when a friend our age suffers a heart attack or if we think about the fact that we've outlived a family member who died of a heart attack. But otherwise, how many of us feel thankful for the heart attacks we didn't have, the cars we didn't wreck, the jobs we didn't take?

Truth is, we tend to get accustomed to our blessings. The other night, right around dusk, I was walking with my wife and kids around our neighborhood. The children had run ahead, chasing some lightning bugs down the street. I stopped there on the sidewalk and just looked around. Years ago I'd prayed for a wife whom I would love and who would love me—and here she was. Years after that, we'd prayed together through infertility and miscarriages for a child—and here they were, four of them, chasing lightning bugs. It wasn't that I'm not grateful, really; it was that this had become the "new normal."

When I was walking down the street with tears streaming down my face, praying for an end to the miscarriages, the blessing I wanted seemed very real to me. When my unmiscarried children are scurrying around my feet, I'm drawn away from seeing just how filled with awe and wonder it is that they're here. The word "daddy" has become far more commonplace than it ever was when I would stay up all night pleading with God to let me hear it, just once, directed to me.

That's what philosophers and psychologists sometimes call "hedonic adaptation."[3] We become accustomed to whatever level of happiness we've achieved, and then we crave whatever's next. You typically aren't really satisfied when you start making the amount of money you want to make, or when you start living in the home you've always wanted, or when you have the family you've prayed for—you just expect things to be that way.

And your aspirations look ahead to what you don't have, yet. This is why we so often see the midlife crisis—and not just among men. A person looks around at some point in life and wonders, "What am I missing?" From the outside you can see what this person can't: "What in the world more could you want?" But that's just the point. This person doesn't know; he or she just wants, period.

In his temptation Jesus recognized what Eve, Israel, and we have not—that cycles of abundance and abasement are part of God's strategic purpose, not because of his ignorance of human need. Israel believed their scarcity of food was evidence that Pharaoh, not God, was their true father. When the manna came, and the quails, they grew sick of the regularity of it all and grumbled for something else. Jesus saw through all of this, though. He recognized that God's discipline isn't hatred but love.

Why was Israel "humbled" with food and with want? It was because God was teaching them not to be Egyptians or Canaanites, slaves of other gods, when they came into their land. If they fell for the illusion of self-provision, they would wind up with stomachs satisfied and hearts "lifted up" (Deut. 8:14). They would then conclude, "My power and the might of my hand have gotten me this wealth" (Deut. 8:17). The cycle would continue then as they would "go after other gods" (Deut. 8:19), seeking to harness their power in order to pile up more and more of the stuff their appetites craved. But God's kingdom will not have the demonic in it; so the end result would be death, being thrown into the fire right along with their idols (Deut. 8:20). Moreover, Jesus understood he was a king-in-training. He knew that a qualification for kingship is control over the appetites (Deut. 17:17), a test previous Israelite kings had failed at one point or another.

Jesus knew that the time of hunger wasn't about punishment but came from God to "humble" and to "test" and "to do you good in the end" (Deut. 8:16). In fatherhood, after all, discipline is itself a part of provision. Just as they didn't have child support attorneys in the biblical world, neither did they have career counselors or corporate internships. A father didn't simply provide his child with food in the child's early life in the home. It was no anomaly that Jesus first found his disciples James and John fishing with their father, Zebedee. That was the way the world worked. A son learned from his father, as did Adam, how to bring forth bread from the ground. The father taught his sons how to carry on the family occupation so that they could provide for their own children.

Jesus pointed out that this, too, is part of the cosmic order: "The Son can do nothing of his own accord, but only what he sees the Father doing" (John 5:19). Jesus understood that discipline isn't God's rejection but his embrace: "Know then in your heart that, as a man disciplines his son, the LORD your God disciplines you" (Deut. 8:5).

If Jesus had commanded the stones to become bread, he would have falsified God's earlier word, "This is my beloved Son." Not only would it have been a kind of paternity test, seeking verification of God's Word, it would have been, as with Eve and Israel, an assertion that Jesus knew better what he needed and when. Jesus would have directed his Father to do what a father should do. He would have disciplined his Father. God forbid.

To lose control of your appetites is to lose sight of the gospel itself, the truth that God knows what you need to survive—the broken body and spilled blood of Jesus. God allows his people to "hunger" so he can feed them with what is better than what they would choose. The Israelites wanted Egyptian onions and leeks; God was training their appetites for bread from heaven.

For most Western Christians gluttony is thought of as a joke rather than as a grave sin. We laugh about our "addictions" to sugar or fat or caffeine. It's true that we're concerned about the relationship between food and our bodies—sometimes hyper-concerned—but usually for health reasons (forestalling diabetes or high blood pressure or other ailments) or for economic reasons (not wanting to pay health care costs for those who overconsume red meat or sugar or alcohol or tobacco) or social, political, or environmental justice reasons. Now all these factors are significant moral aspects of eating. But there are also the personal, spiritual costs of gluttony, and that's hard for us to see.

Gluttony is not equated simply with obesity. After all, one with a fast metabolism could consume an entire pecan pie and still look scrawny while another might eat with a rigid scrupulosity and still be, as folks would put it where I grew up, "big boned" due to genetic factors. The issue isn't the size of the person, necessarily, but the rule of the appetites.

Gluttony would sometimes include, I think, what we often think of today as eating disorders. Some fall into the compulsion to "gain control" over some area of life by refusing food (which God says is necessary and good) or by indulging and then vomiting up the contents in a kind of nutritional onanism. This isn't to say that eating disorders are easily solved with a spiritually stern admonition to stop. There are often deep and complex psychological and physiological factors at play. But often the eating disorders we see, even in our churches, are evidence of an appetite (sometimes the appetite to conform to societal expectations of body size) gaining sovereignty over a life.

The discipline of the body over food, which God designed through cycles of both fasting and feasting, is necessary to recognize God's fatherly goodness and sovereignty. That's what Mardi Gras in relation to Lent gets right. No person's appetite is sovereign. It is balanced out by the larger considerations of worship, life, culture, family, society. A life that is all fast or all feast is disordered to the core.

Food is connected in almost every human culture with sex. American culture has exported around the world restaurants in which women in tight-fitting shirts and skirts sell processed chicken breasts while offering men the opportunity to ogle their breasts. Both appetites are to be whetted, and at least one of them is filled. This connection is twisted, but it isn't accidental. The Bible asserts it, often.

Notice that Esau traded in his birthright for a meal, and yet the book of Hebrews uses this incident to warn against being "sexually immoral or unholy like Esau" (12:16). But, unless I've forgotten a naked woman rolling around somewhere in that narrative, Esau wasn't sexually immoral in the Genesis text. He ate a meal. The apostle Paul connects the Israelite wilderness grumblings about food and water to their idolatry and to their "sexual immorality" (1 Cor. 10:8; Num. 25:1–9). Why is this? In the Christian view of the world, there's a direct connection between food and sex all the way from that time when the taste of a fruit led to immediate genital shame (Gen. 3:6–7).

Sex, like food, is a built-in appetite. Now the sex instinct isn't the same kind of appetite as an appetite for food. Food is necessary for all human life, whereas sexual intercourse isn't. No one will die without sexual release (regardless of what adolescent and post-adolescent boys may try to tell their girlfriends), whereas without food or water the human body cannot continue to exist. The necessity is there, though. An individual can exist without sexual intercourse, but a family line cannot, and the human race cannot.

And sex demonstrates for us, regularly, how primal the appetite can be. A starving man can show how irrational the food drive can make one—killing and stealing for it—but rarely are people truly starving. The sex instinct can make you feel like you are "starving" and make you willing to risk as much as an emaciated man is willing to risk looting a grocery store to feed himself. Moreover, sex—like food—is a creation structure designed to point humanity toward something beyond the creation itself. The sexual union is not simply a rubbing of parts together; it is a "profound mystery" that forms a biological and spiritual union that points to God's archetypal plan for the communion of Christ and his church (Eph. 5:32). This is why I think one contemporary scholar is quite right when she speaks of a lack of self-control in this area as "sexual obesity."[4]

Sexual infidelity (and by this I mean any sexual liaison outside of the one-flesh marriage union) isn't dangerous primarily because of its temporal consequences. These consequences are quite real, of course, and they are devastating. It is dangerous because it repudiates the gospel, molests the icon of Christ and his church, and forms another, malevolent spiritual union that cannot be disentangled when the situation is left behind.

In our time pornography has become the destroying angel of male Eros. I don't mean to suggest that pornography is only a male temptation (it is not), but pornography, because of the way a man has been designed toward arousal, is, when available, a universal male temptation. It has come to the point now that whenever I meet with a couple in which there is a man who is an emotional shell of himself—dead to intimacy with his wife—and a marriage is fraying apart, I ask how long the pornography has been going on. In every case it's there.

There is a kind of helplessness that a man engaged in pornography exhibits. He often speaks of it in terms of a "struggle" or an "addiction." Now both of those terms are accurate, I believe, but they distance a person from his sin in a soul-decaying manner. Pornography is not just an addiction; it is occultism. The man who sits upstairs viewing pornography while his wife chauffeurs the kids to soccer practice is not some unusual "pervert"; he is (like his forefather Adam) seeking the mystery of the universe apart from Christ. That's the reason the one picture, stored in his memory, of that naked woman will never be enough for him. He will never be able to be satisfied because he will never be able to get an image naked enough.

I say pornography is occultism because I believe the draw

toward it is more than biological (though that is strong). The satanic powers understand that "the sexually immoral person sins against his own body" (1 Cor. 6:18). They understand that the pornographic act severs a one-flesh marriage union at the very point of intimate connectedness and instead joins Christ, spiritually, to an electronic prostitute (1 Cor. 6:16). They also know that those who unrepentantly practice such things "will not inherit the kingdom of God" (1 Cor. 6:9–10).

Pornography is, in one sense, no different from any other form of sexual temptation. But in another sense it is even more insidious. Pornography brings with it a kind of pseudo-repentance. Immediately after it is "over," the participant feels a kind of revulsion and self-loathing. Whereas an adulterer or a fornicator can at least rationalize a kind of transcendent "love" behind his sin, even a conscience thoroughly seared over rarely wants to write love songs or poetry in celebration of his pornographic self-satisfaction.

Typically—at least in those who have some sort of Christian or moral identity—the pornographic act is followed by a resolve never to do it again, to leave it behind and find some sort of accountability. But what masquerades as a repentant conscience is in most cases little more than a sated appetite. When the appetite is "hungry" once again, the demonic powers will collaborate with the biological impulses to find a way to make it seem irresistible again. As the cycle of temptation grinds on, the illusion of repentance keeps the sin in hiding, so that actual repentance never happens until, as with Esau, the conscience is so seared that repentance is then impossible (Heb. 6:4–6; 12:16–17).

This is, of course, exactly where the powers want any child of Adam—and especially any professing brother or sister of the Lord Jesus. Jesus flees Satan's temptation not because he doesn't like bread, but because he wants more bread than Satan can provide and because he wants the bread in fellowship with his Father and with his bride. The Devil wants a masturbatory meal, wolfed down alone in the desert. Jesus wants a marriage supper, joined with his church "as a bride adorned for her husband" (Rev. 21:2) in the New Jerusalem.

As I mentioned above, women are certainly susceptible to sexual immorality—fornication, adultery, and even pornography. Women who would be thoroughly disgusted by visual representations of graphic genital activity are sometimes captured by a not-altogether-different medium of lust and covetousness. Romance has, of course, always been a part of human literature. But so has sex. And just as there's a difference between the erotic energy of, say, the Song of Solomon or *Romeo and Juliet* and hard-core raunch, there's a vast distinction between romance depicted in art and "art" that is designed merely for the purpose of titillating the appetite for emotional intimacy. Pornography "works" for those who "consume" it because it's built on an illusion, the illusion of a perfectly willing, perfectly aroused partner without the "work" of relational intimacy. Often romance novels or their film equivalents do the same thing for the emotional needs of women that pornography offers for the erotic urges of men.

Thankfully, we do not have a market for "Christian" pornography yet (but just wait, someone will find a way), but we do have a market for "Christian" romance novels. Now some of those so classified aren't really "romance novels" at all. They are complicated looks at the human condition—especially the male/female relationship—from a Christian vantage point. But a lot of this genre is simply a Christianization of a form that's intended not to examine intimacy but to escape to an artificial illusion of it. Granted, there's no graphic sexuality here. The hero and the heroine don't sleep together; they pray together. But that's just the point. How many disappointed middle-aged women in our congregations are reading these novels as a means of comparing the strong spiritual leaders depicted there with what by comparison must seem to be underachieving lumps lying next to them on the couch? This is not to equate "romance novels" with the grave soul destruction of pornography, but it is worth asking, "Is what I'm consuming leading me toward contentment with my husband (or future husband) or away from it?"

In Western global culture, food is assumed. Disconnected from the agrarian context that most people in every culture would have taken for granted, we now assume, almost literally, that bread appears from the stones of the ground, since so few of us have anything to do with tilling and working the ground. It is a bit odd for us to hear the crowds demanding bread from Jesus in John 6, since it sounds to us akin to asking for a snack at a sporting event. Bread was for ancient Israelite culture (and for that matter almost every culture) the basic engine of economic survival. The first temptation is not just about consuming food; it is about consuming, period. It is about our quest for economic security, our appetite for stuff.

Covetousness is, again, something subtle and not easy to detect in our lives. A man who walks into his church account-ability group and starts rubbing his hands together with glee describing the rear end of the woman he saw on the beach last week will (in most churches) be immediately rebuked by some-one with some spiritual maturity. A man who does the same thing about the boat he saw at the beach last week will probably simply be engaged in further conversation. But the burning to acquire things is devilish and leads to misery and ruin.

"For the love of money is a root of all kinds of evils," the apostle Paul writes. "It is through this craving that some have wandered away from the faith and pierced themselves with many pangs" (1 Tim. 6:10). It is, Paul says, a "desire to be rich" that is a "temptation," "a snare," that leads "into many senseless and harmful desires that plunge people into ruin and destruc-tion" (1 Tim. 6:9).

Unfortunately, our perception is so skewed by our context that we assume that the "desire to be rich" is the desire to be the kind of multimillionaire with which we're so familiar in our culture. The definition of "rich" in Scripture doesn't even contemplate such hyperwealth. It is instead economic freedom, security. The riches described about Nebuchadnezzar and Herod and the oppressors "fattened" by luxury and self-indulgence in Amos and James are far less luxurious than what one would see in a working-class American household today.

The Scripture does not forbid wealth, and the Scripture indeed mandates a certain kind of economic self-sufficiency (within the context of the larger tribe and society). A man who does not provide for his family "is worse than an unbeliever" (1 Tim. 5:8). The gospel compels us away from idleness and to "toil and labor" for our bread (2 Thess. 3:8). But the appetite for things is as insatiable as the appetite for food and sex and can be just as deadly.

The biblical mandate is never to set a certain standard of living to which all believers must conform as an external code, but there certainly is biblical warrant in noting the danger of temptation that comes along with great wealth. It is hardly legalism to ask such questions as, how much of this do we need? and how much are we giving away? and so on.[5] A hermeneutic of suspicion about our own wealth combined with a gratitude for what God has given us can converge in a Spirit weapon against covetousness. Through it we can recognize that "love of money" and hoarding of stuff is less a lifestyle than a persistently asked question—"Is the LORD among us or not?" (Ex. 17:7), or in other words, "If I am really the son of God . . . ." The Spirit of Christ compels us toward contentment. We are able to be free from the love of money when we recognize our identity and our inheritance in Christ and cling to the promise, "I will never leave you nor forsake you" (Heb. 13:5).

Self-control is, in this fallen world, counterintuitive and countercultural, so much so that anyone possessing it will seem bizarre if not subversive. That's especially true for those of us living in an era of unparalleled affluence, in which there is the illusion of a limitlessness of conceivable consumption. This has changed the makeup and witness of our churches, I fear, in ways that are mostly invisible to us. We have become the people Jesus warned us about—fat, upwardly mobile, and politically influential. In the meantime we've become accommodated in almost every way to the culture that surrounds us. We must recognize that one of the roots of the family crisis around us—in the pews we sit in or preach to every week—is the wallet in our own back pocket.

Too many of our churches, too many of us, have made peace with the sexual revolution and the familial chaos left in its wake precisely because we made peace, long before, with the love of money. We wish to live with the same standard of living as the culture around us (there is no sin in that), but we are willing to get there by any means necessary.

Why does the seemingly godly church member in one of our congregations or parishes drive his pregnant teenage daughter to the nearest city under cover of darkness to obtain an abortion? Because no matter how much he "votes his values," when crisis hits, he wants his daughter to have a "normal" life. He is pro-life with, as one feminist leader put it, three exceptions—rape, incest, and my situation.[6]

Why do Christian parents, contra Saint Paul's clear admonition in 1 Corinthians 7, encourage their young adult children to delay marriage, sometimes for years past the time it would take to discern whether this union would be of the Lord? Why do we smilingly tell them to wait until they can "afford" it? It is because, to our shame, we deem fornication a less awful reality than financial hardship.

Why do our pastors and church leaders speak bluntly about homosexuality but not about divorce, despite the fact that evangelical Christian divorce rates are the same or higher than those in the world we consider "unchurched"?[7] It is because in many cases church leaders know the faces of the divorced people in the pews before them, and they fear losing the membership statistics or the revenue those faces represent.[8] To put it bluntly, we have many more out-of-the-closet multiple divorcées than out-of-the-closet homosexuals in our churches. John the Baptist put his head on a platter to speak the truth that not even a king can claim another man's wife. John the Modern Evangelical isn't willing to put his retirement benefits on the table to say the same thing to a congregational business meeting.

For many Christians, divorce does not seem like a culture-war issue because it is not shocking or disgusting. We have grown accustomed to our "one spouse at a time" world. Now we don't celebrate divorce, of course. But we see it as a personal tragedy, not as a scandal in our witness to the gospel. And we will have grandchildren and great-grandchildren for whom sex reassignment surgeries, prostitution, and polygamy may seem just as "tragic but normal" as divorce seems to us. Will they be more countercultural than we? We have become slow-train sexual revolutionaries, embracing sexual anarchy a generation after the broader culture has done so. Our grandchildren's sins are denounced because our grandchildren aren't there to hear it, and our grandchildren don't pay the bills. It's the exact same demographic profiling strategy Madison Avenue uses with advertising; it's just that the demographic is different.

Why do we speak endlessly about marital communication and "love languages" but never address the question of whether institutionalized day care is good for children or for their parents? It's because pastors know that couples would reply that they could never afford to live on the provision of the husband alone. And they're almost always right—if living means living in the neighborhoods in which they now live with the technologies they now have. Why do we never ask whether it might be better to live in a one-bedroom apartment or a trailer park than to outsource the rearing of one's children? It's because the American way of life seems so normal to us that such things do not even seem to be options at all.

When confronted with the challenge of a countercultural, life-affirming (but economically less acquisitive) life, too often we see what our inerrant Bibles define as the joyful life but walk away saddened. Here we're just like another rich young man (though he would be poor compared to literally almost anyone reading this page right now) who wanted eternal life but wanted his possessions more (Luke 18:18–30).

Here contemporary Christians could stand to listen to some of our more secular liberal critics, who deny a biblical understanding of reality but who seem to understand the connection between the whirl of personal destruction and the corporate culture we take for granted. After all, they are not usually Greenwich Village bohemians in tie-dye shirts or ecofeminist Marxists with Darwin fish on their Volkswagen vans who produce the cultural pornotopia that America is now exporting around the world and right into the addresses listed in our church directories. The money behind this stuff is more likely from "conservatives" in traditional-cut suits, and some of them know what a baptistery looks like from the inside and how to tell a hymn from a praise chorus.

Too often Christians assume that consumer culture is morally neutral and that American corporatism must be godly, since it is opposed so strongly by the culture warriors of the Left. But the counterculture there is an illusion. Both the Left and the Right in the American mainstream are captive to the ideology that the appetites are to be indulged by whatever system will do it most efficiently.

Philosophers Joseph Heath and Andrew Potter are correct that the counterculture and the consumer culture are symbiotic. As they put it, "In the end, it is just people fighting for their right to party."[9] We should ask, then, whether consumer activist Ralph Nader is right that television advertising is a threat to the family order, since "corporations have decided that kids under twelve are a lucrative market, and they sell directly to them, subverting parental authority."[10] Is it any wonder then that most of us have seen films our grandparents would have deemed pornographic? Perhaps it is true that our grandparents were too prudish and hyperscrupulous about such things. Or perhaps we are living in a situation in which those who make a living off feeding our appetites are feeding our appetites, and we've never even noticed.

The church can take on the tyranny of the appetites not simply by pointing out what in our cultural milieu is inconsistent with the gospel, but by presenting a positive alternative, a counterculture in which the transitory nature of momentary self-satisfaction is transcended by a seeking first of the kingdom of God. This is about more than just preaching (although it certainly encompasses that).

Novelist John Updike once wrote, "America is a vast conspiracy to make you happy."[11] Contemporary American evangelicalism is a vast conspiracy to sell each other stuff. If we're ever going to model that man does not live by bread alone, we must resist the fact that Christianity has become a marketing niche for faraway corporate bureaucrats with a bottom line to maintain.

What if our churches actively stood against the advertising culture by, for instance, cultivating our own musical culture rather than simply importing whatever is filtered down from the Christian music "industry"? There was a day when Christian musical expression—from Byzantine chant to Appalachian bluegrass—bubbled up to the culture from the folk forms of local congregations. It could be that way again. Perhaps we wouldn't sound as "professional" if we called out our people and worked to disciple them in the musical arts—whether in harp or in voice or in steel guitar—and allowed their creativity to find its niche within our congregational life, just as we do with preaching and teaching. We'd have some bad music in a lot of our churches. But would it be any worse than the endless "worship" leadership we see now, imitating whatever has been market tested long enough to make it on the so-called Christian airwaves?

What if our churches opted out of the Christian celebrity racket? There will, of course, always be leaders to whom the churches will look. It has been so since the New Testament (James, Peter, Paul, Clement, and the list goes on and on). But isn't it worth having the conversation that your pastor doesn't need to be whoever the most faddish preacher of the moment is in order to be a blessing to your church? What if rather than simply buying more and more small-group curricula, your congregation tried—as an experiment—teaching and training some within the church how to do some of that? Not all of it, of course. I'm not suggesting that.

There is a diversity of gifts within the larger body of Christ, just as there is within each local congregation, and it would be counterproductive and redundant not to use materials that are available. But we could find small mutinous ways to say to the industries that often ply us with stuff to buy, "We live by the *Logos*, not by your logo."

A church that sees, and rejects, the first temptation will do more than simply implement emphases to educate people away from acquisitiveness. It will embrace an entirely new ethos, away from the spirit of the age. The idea of the church as one more product in a free market is unquestioned. One leading evangelical figure of the late generation, as quoted by a journalist hostile to conservative Christianity, compared the church experience he sought with the experience of changing toothpaste brands "just for the fun of it." The pastor says that we all must admit that when we do this we feel a "secret little thrill" as questions run through our minds: "Will it make my teeth whiter? My breath fresher?" Now I may just be odd, but I've never had even one "excited question" run through my mind when buying toothpaste. I have to admit (and feel free to correct me if I'm wrong here) that I find it hard to believe anyone actually experiences that kind of "excitement" buying toothpaste except in a television commercial. But his larger point is that churches should "harness the forces of free-market capitalism in our ministry" since people "like the benefits, risks, and maybe above all, the excitement of a free-market society."[12] But how is that working out for us?

Whatever our views on what we typically think of as "the economy" (that is, the right ordering of government to the market, etc.), surely we can agree that the economic order within the church is to be different, even from temporal orders we believe to be good and just. After all, most of us agree that some form of a democratic republic is the best temporal political system, and yet the church is not a democracy but a Christocracy. Even those of us who hold to congregational church government don't believe the authority rests "of, by, and for the people" but in the rule of Christ as expressed through his Word and Spirit. Even if a consumer-oriented free market economy, on one side, or a centrally planned welfare state economy, on the other, is what you want in your government, it is not what we should want in our churches. The customer or the consumer or the constituent, within the church, doesn't best know what he needs or even, ultimately, what he wants. The Father God does.

In a wide-ranging critique of the contemporary political economy, Wendell Berry notes, "A society in which every school child 'needs' a computer and every sixteen-year-old 'needs' an automobile, and every eighteen-year-old 'needs' to go to college is already delusional and is well on its way to being broke."[13] Berry calls for an "inverting" of the economy so that consumption is not the highest good. Whether or not you agree that would be a good idea for the global economic order—and whether or not you think it is possible to get there from here—it certainly is, I think, both advisable and possible to "invert" the economies of local churches—away from consumption of spiritual goods and services as the highest good and toward something simpler, something deeper, something older.

Often critiques of consumerist church life are directed toward so-called seeker-friendly, suburban megachurches. But this is hardly fair. First, the size of a congregation has little to do with its vision of the good. Moreover, many of these critiques come from churches and ministries just as consumerist, just directed toward a different demographic market. Thus churches with linear, analytical thinkers tend to be doctrinally heavy in the most rational and intellectual kind of way. The seekers are there, targeted and marketed to, all with the same range of thickness in their eyeglasses. The same is true of worship, church government, or any other range of issues. Moreover, often the most scathing critiques of larger so-called consumerist churches come from congregations envious of the "success" of the larger churches around them. But one cannot with integrity critique consumerism from the standpoint of covetousness—the very problem with consumerism *is* the covetousness.

Certain aspects of what is derided as consumerism—being kind to guests, welcoming children, clear signage, friendly communication—is less about marketing than about simple neighbor-love. And there are aspects of covetousness and acquisitiveness that show up even in the most self-consciously nonconsumerist churches and ministries. Moreover, we must recognize the legitimacy of the appetites; man does live by bread. A church that doesn't recognize felt needs doesn't care anything about people. There's a difference, though, between an appetite-driven ministry and a ministry that transforms by redirecting the appetites.

How many of our churches, I wonder, appeal to carnal appetites alone as the means by which we might someday be able to introduce others to the lordship of Christ? Jesus doesn't work in this way. When Jesus multiplied the loaves of bread, the satisfied appetites on the seashore were willing to announce Jesus' kingship. As a matter of fact, they not only professed it, they "were about to come and take him by force to make him king" (John 6:15). But Jesus left. Maybe he still does.

Moreover, in our one-on-one discipleship, churches must model what it means to take the appetites seriously. The primary thrust of what a tempted Christ does in us, though, isn't negative but positive. Jesus, through the Holy Spirit, doesn't just free us from our appetites by crucifying them with him; he also enables us to walk in the freedom of his newness of life.

The ultimate antidote to self-provision, and the ultimate fuel for self-control, is gratitude. Gratitude isn't about God's ego. It is about our discipline, our being shaped into the kind of men and women who can be kings and queens over the universe. We can only inherit that kingdom as little children (Matt. 18:4), that is, as those who have a receptivity to blessing. We embrace God's discipline, feasting when he feeds our appetites, waiting when he doesn't, because we know he is working to do us good in the end.

It's true that gratitude and contentment and self-control don't stop your stomach from grumbling. You want what you want. But the discipline of God teaches you, slowly, to put old appetites to death and to whet new ones. Through the Spirit of Christ you learn to crucify "the flesh with its passions and desires" (Gal. 5:24). That's hard. It usually means hunger or economic want or sexual frustration or familial longing. But through it we learn to see that life is about more than acquisition—whether acquisition of possessions or orgasms or pleasant memories. The temporary hunger can cause us, with our Lord Jesus in the wilderness temptations, to turn away from momentary satisfaction—whether of our culinary or sexual or consumer "needs"—and toward the more permanent things.

CONCLUSION

On the morning after Mardi Gras it's easy to feel the queasiness of stomach, the pounding of the hangover, or the throbbing of the conscience. It's much harder to feel the futility of a whole life lived under the tyranny of the appetites. That's especially true when, as with most of us, we see the sovereignty of our appetites as normal. We live among a people, let's be honest, whose stomachs are full but who are vomiting it all up with an Esau-like disgust. We live in a culture of craving that is never satisfied, in a world where it is always Mardi Gras and never Easter.

But Jesus has hungered with us, and for us. He is the first-born son of the kingdom, the true humanity, and the true Israel of God. Jesus understood what his fathers in the garden and in the wilderness didn't. When confronted with the question, "Are you the Son of God?" he heard the word of his Father more loudly than the word of his own grumbling stomach.

Our enemy doesn't outwit Jesus. Jesus isn't deceived into thinking that because man lives by bread (which is true), man then lives by bread alone (which isn't). Jesus understood the appetites and how they fit in the larger picture of the mystery of man's creatureliness and human dignity. He wouldn't question his Father's provision, even though he couldn't see it at the time.

Through the Spirit of Christ, the same becomes true of us. The fear of death overshadows us, tempting us to grab what we want, to satisfy our cravings, before we lose our opportunity. The reign of death seeks to drive us on to fill our guts with what we think we need. In order to follow Jesus through this wilderness, though, we must learn to be fathered as well as fed. In order to get to the Father's table, we must end the grip that death has on us by teaching us to crave more and more of what cannot satisfy. We must starve to death.

4

FREE FALLING

Why We'd Rather Be Right Than Rescued

The noise-canceling earphones worked even better than I imagined they would. I was wedged in a seat on an airplane, right next to a snoring accountant and right in front of a screaming infant. The woman in the seat across the aisle was giving, last I heard, a discourse on how the doctors successfully treated her bladder infection. But I couldn't hear a bit of it. The headset was so soundproof that it created a virtual sonic cocoon, shutting off everything except the music I carried with me. I couldn't even hear myself. And that was the problem.

At some point in the flight, I noticed everyone in front of me looking back with looks of incredulity on their faces. For that nanosecond I intuited all kinds of scary scenarios. Maybe there was a hole blown out of the back of the plane, whipping passengers behind us out the vacuum. Maybe a terrorist was back there with a gun to a woman's head and a note demanding a trip to Cuba and some cash. Before any other possibility could form in my mind, I turned around, only to see everyone behind me looking forward with that same look of confused horror.

That's when I realized, "Oh my word, they're looking at me." And one second later I recognized that I'd been singing the song "Free Falling" with great volume and enthusiasm, but couldn't hear myself. My fellow travelers could, though, and I guess they didn't like it. Maybe it was my voice, maybe it was the lyrics; we'll never know for sure.

I blushed and cringed. There's really nothing to say at a time like that. You just tell yourself it could be much worse and that you'll never see these people again. You try to retreat into an even deeper cocoon than the one you were in before. You're humiliated. You're exposed. You're vulnerable. There's a kind of natural fight-or-flight reaction that wells up from somewhere inside you. It's terrible.

You've probably felt that way. Now it probably wasn't due to an impromptu concert in a public venue, but you've probably felt vulnerable. There's a reason, after all, why lots of people dream about taking a major exam on a subject they haven't studied or why others dream of realizing as they walk through their work or school that they forgot to put on pants. For some of you it was the fear of speaking your lines in front of all those people in that class play. For some of you it was the fear of fumbling the football in that key play in the last quarter of the game of your life. For some of you it was the fear of going in to see your supervisor for your annual performance review. The possibility of being exposed, and publicly embarrassed, is an almost universal human fear. And we seek to protect ourselves from exposure, from embarrassment, and ultimately from harm—sometimes by any means necessary.

For others of you there's something in your background that has left you with something far more terrifying than humiliation to be afraid of. Maybe you were abused or raped or beaten. Maybe there's an addiction out there you're afraid will come back to grab you by the throat. Maybe there's a genetic disease in your family, and you're constantly watching to see if—or when—it shows up on your own medical charts. You want protection. This is the second temptation of Christ.[1]

The second temptation is in many ways the most difficult one for Christians to understand. Most of us, after all, can sympathize with wanting to wolf down some bread when you're hungry, and most of us can identify with the pull to be ruler of the world. It's hard to see, though, what's alluring about jumping off a tower. True, I've known people who have told me that they think, when looking down from the Empire State Building, about what it would be like to jump. And some have told me they get the chilling thought of veering into oncoming traffic sometimes when they drive down a crowded highway. But these are easy to recognize as somewhat disturbed and at least borderline suicidal. It doesn't, though, seem like a temptation that is "common to man" (1 Cor. 10:13). But it is. And if you and I are ever going to find the security we crave, we'll have to see why, in our fallenness, we'd rather be right than rescued.

A QUESTION OF VERIFICATION

In order to grasp something of what was happening here, let's step back and notice the geography. We don't know how much time had elapsed between Jesus' test with the stones and this one, but at some point the unclean spirit of the desert took Jesus to Jerusalem, to the highest point of the temple itself. Whether this was a physical transportation or some kind of mystical vision, again we aren't told. Somehow Jesus in the rocky wilderness found himself in Jerusalem, as the apostle Paul would put it, "whether in the body or out of the body I do not know" (2 Cor. 12:2).

As the wind whipped through his hair, Jesus looked down from the dizzying heights to hear the devilish voice say to him, "If you are the Son of God, throw yourself down" (Matt. 4:6). What is perhaps of most importance in this offer are the words Luke includes in his narration: "Throw yourself down *from here*" (Luke 4:9).

"Here" was Jerusalem, and "here" was the temple. This isn't incidental. Jerusalem was far more than just a capital city or even a religious Mecca for the Jews. Jerusalem was the City of the Great King, the place where God had promised to put his name and his presence. And the temple was far more than a cathedral or denominational headquarters. The temple was the dwelling place of God himself. God committed to be with his people, and he did so in such a way that he could be with them visibly—first through the cloud and the fire leading them out of Egypt, then in the traveling tent of the tabernacle during their wilderness wanderings, and finally, after they'd come into the land, in a building he'd directed the house of David to construct for him, in which he would dwell.

God's holy presence in his temple is why Jesus' contemporaries were so shocked and appalled when he would say things like, "Destroy this temple, and in three days I will raise it up" (John 2:19). This wasn't, to them, the equivalent of our hearing someone say, "Blow up St. Louis Cathedral or First Baptist Dallas and I'll reconstruct it." It was far more blasphemous than that. The temple was where God was. You didn't approach it lightly. You certainly didn't draw near to the Most Holy Place, where the manifest presence of God was. Satan took Jesus to this place.

As he looked down, Jesus would have seen quite a contrast from the silence of the desert rocks. He could probably see people buzzing in and out of the marketplaces. He could probably see children playing in the streets. There below him were Abraham's children, just as God had promised, as numerous as the sands of the seashore. Jesus could see David's city all around him being governed by a foreign power, the uncircumcised Romans. Like Moses on the mountaintop, Jesus could see from here both the "already" and the "not yet" of God's kingdom promise.

As Jesus looked at the drop below, Satan whispered—or maybe he roared—the words "Throw yourself down." This wasn't a threat or a taunt or a dare. This was a sermon. Satan was preaching a biblical text, citing part of Psalm 91, verse by verse. Here Satan showed his gift, once again, as an expository Bible preacher. For one thing, it wasn't only Jesus who had memorized the Scriptures. So had Satan. He recited a Psalm from memory, and recited it with accuracy. Moreover, Satan didn't just know the proof text—he knew the larger canonical context. He knew to apply this reference to God's ultimate anointed, to Jesus. Satan was, in this instance, a Christ-centered Bible preacher too.

Psalm 91 is a song about God's protection and man's fear: "He who dwells in the shelter of the Most High will abide in the shadow of the Almighty" (v. 1). Through a whirl of metaphors, the Psalm compares God's deliverance of his anointed in terms of a rescuer of captured birds, a bird covering his young with his wings, a shield fending off an opponent's arrows, and so on. The certainty of God's deliverance ought to prompt the anointed away from fear: "You will not fear the terror of the night, nor the arrow that flies by day, nor the pestilence that stalks in darkness, nor the destruction that wastes at noonday" (vv. 5–6).

After forty days in the desert surely Jesus would have resonated with those words. Can you imagine sleeping in the black night of a Judean wild place, with no street lamps or security lights, nothing but moonlight, starlight, and blackness all around? How would it be to sleep not knowing when, at any moment, you could feel the hot panting of a beast's tongue right before your face as it called a pack of others together to rip your veins from your throat? And as the church's desert fathers would write centuries later, just as bad as the uncertainty of the night could be that "noonday destruction," the sense of hopelessness and meaninglessness that could come when the sun is at its highest.[2]

But at this time and in this place, the biblical promise just wouldn't have seemed to be true. The Bible reassures the anointed, after all, that "no evil shall be allowed to befall you, no plague come near your tent" (Ps. 91:10). And yet here Jesus was in the presence of the lord of the flies, the prince of darkness. What could possibly be more of a plague or pestilence than that?

Satan the preacher continued his exposition. Jesus could jump, he offered, because the Bible was true. He cited from the psalmist's lyrics: "For he will command his angels concerning you to guard you in all your ways. On their hands they will bear you up, lest you strike your foot against a stone" (Ps. 91:11–12). Of course, Jesus knew about the angels. These mysterious creatures were there with him in the desert, and at the end of this round of testing they would be visible to him (Mark 1:13). Satan prompted Jesus to force their visibility now.

What Satan was seeking to entice Jesus to do was to prove something, to test out a hypothesis. Jesus' body sailing over the edge of the pinnacle would verify, first of all, that the Word of God about God's protecting presence was true. Second, it would verify that this protective presence was true as it relates to Jesus particularly. As the plummeting Galilean was swooped upward from the perilous ground below, he would see, with his eyes, the answer to the implied question in the words, "If you are the Son of God . . ."

Again we must come back to the question of why Jesus would be drawn to such a thing. This was, after all, a real temptation. There was a struggle here, a submitting of Jesus' will to his Father's. Jesus was experiencing this precisely as we do, except without sin. So what does Jesus want here? Quite simply, Jesus the man wanted what every son and daughter wants—to be safe and to be loved.

Satan's offer here was one more assault on God's fatherhood and on Jesus' sonship. "If you are the Son of God," he said, "throw yourself down." Fathers do not merely provide for their children—feeding them; they also protect their children from external threat—fighting for them and protecting them.

When our oldest sons were babies, we were probably a little more protective of them than what I would counsel a parent to be now. We had adopted them from a Russian orphanage, and we were working, little by little, to get them adjusted to life in a family. At the time their cribs were in a bedroom on the main floor of the house, while my wife's and my bedroom was in the basement area below. We felt terribly guilty about being on two separate floors, but, this being the way the house was made, we lived with it, putting an electronic baby monitor in their room and in ours so that we could hear if they needed us.

One evening in the middle of the night, I awakened to hear a strange man's voice on the baby monitor, saying, "Do you know what I'm about to do?" Half asleep, I bolted from the bed and ran up the stairs. With a pounding heartbeat and shaking hands, I leaped up and kicked in the door to their bedroom, taking on some kind of kung-fu maneuver that is wholly unnatural to me. I heard myself screaming, "If you touch them, I will kill you."

There was no one there. We later learned that the baby monitor signal had picked up someone's telephone conversation. Now I had two screaming babies who knew just enough English to wonder, I'm sure, why their new daddy was in their room hollering, "I'm going to kill you." Our adjustment to the family plan was set back at least two weeks because of all of that. My reaction, though, was perfectly natural (not the kung-fu moves; there was nothing natural about that). As a father I have a built-in zeal to see my family protected from harm.

That, too, is part of the divine fatherhood to which we all must respond. In the exodus, God fought for his "son," the nation of Israel, ripping them from the clutches of Pharaoh, leading them safely through the perils of the water. In the case of the "sons of God," the kings of Israel, God demonstrated his acceptance of them by fighting for them, protecting them from their warring enemies on every side. It is good to be protected by one's Father, to pray "deliver us from evil" (Matt. 6:13).

Jesus again turned to the words of Deuteronomy. Instead of engaging the serpent-king's expositions point by point, Jesus simply said, "Again it is written, 'You shall not put the Lord your God to the test'" (Matt. 4:7; cf. Luke 4:12). This citation was a signal, a signal that Jesus was not ignorant of what was going on here. There was, after all, in his quotation a larger context. The full citation of this Scripture is:

> You shall not put the LORD your God to the test, as you tested him at Massah. You shall diligently keep the commandments of the LORD your God, and his testimonies and his statutes, which he has commanded you. And you shall do what is right and good in the sight of

the LORD, that it may go well with you, and that you may go in and take possession of the good land that the LORD swore to give to your fathers by thrusting out all your enemies from before you, as the LORD has promised. (Deut. 6:16–19)

"As you tested him at Massah," the Bible said. Something happened at a place called Massah, a spirit Jesus saw afoot in this temptation too. What was it? *Massah* is a word that simply means "testing." This incident took place shortly after God's miraculous provision of the bread from the skies. The people of Israel then faced yet another threat in their desert trek—a lack of water to drink. As the peril grew more pronounced, the people "quarreled" with Moses, the Bible says (Ex. 17:2, 7), demanding that he direct God to bring forth water. Moses recognized that what was going on in this grumbling was a "test" of Israel's God by Israel's people. The people wanted a sign in order to answer a question: "Is the LORD among us or not?" (Ex. 17:7). The question was whether God was right or Pharaoh was right, whether they were really sons or just slaves after all.

I notice that I just wrote that the people wanted a sign from God, but that's not quite right. The people wanted *another* sign from God. God had, after all, given them multiple signs, starting with their initial deliverance from Egypt: "We were Pharaoh's slaves in Egypt. And the LORD brought us out of Egypt with a mighty hand. And the LORD showed signs and wonders, great and grievous, against Egypt and against Pharaoh and all his household, before our eyes" (Deut. 6:21–22).

The people of Israel had seen sign after sign, enough in fact to make them tremble and weep and plead to see no more. But when they faced jeopardy, when the water ran out, they were right back to sign mongering.

This demand for protection was a signal of unbelief. The people didn't trust God, on the basis of his Word, to protect them and deliver them from their enemies. They wanted some visible manifestation, something that would prove that God was a Father after all. At Massah the sign they wanted was a stream of water. But it would later be other things. The addiction to signs is not easily overcome. They wanted to put God on trial, to make him prove whether he was there and whether he was for them on the basis of something more visible than his Word. "Today, if you hear his voice, do not harden your hearts, as at Meribah, as on the day at Massah in the wilderness," the Psalm sings, "when your fathers put me to the test and put me to the proof, though they had seen my work" (Ps. 95:7–9).

The problem for Israel was that they weren't really able to put God to the test. In reality the Israelites were backing up into a story even older than theirs. Eve, after all, was offered the fruit as a means of protection. Her eating it was a challenge as to whether God was correct when he said that in the day they ate of it they would surely die (Gen. 3:3–4). And after eating it, sin led her and her husband to seek further protection from God himself in the vegetation of the garden (Gen. 3:8). They were testing the sovereignty of God.

At Massah the Israelites themselves were actually being tested. In their grumbling sign seeking, God demonstrated that they had gone "astray in their heart, and they have not known my ways" (Ps. 95:10). The end result was God's declaration, "I swore in my wrath, 'They shall not enter my rest'" (Ps. 95:11).

It is no accident that Jesus relived the water test of Massah from atop the temple. The temple is all about water. The prophet Ezekiel envisioned a future temple in which water would trickle out, gradually pick up depth, and ultimately flow out as a mighty river, teeming with life, until it poured out at the roots of the Tree of Life (Ezek. 47:1–12). This water, Jesus said, is "living water" that refreshes forever (John 4:1–30; 7:37–39). Jesus didn't seek to prove the voice of God; he just believed it.

Jesus saw through the satanic deception precisely what neither Eve nor Israel could see. He knew that testing God would mean disqualification from God's people, from the inheritance of "entering my rest." Jesus' name, after all, is literally Joshua. Like the first Joshua, Jesus doesn't require a certainty of visible victory before marching through the enemy's camp. He hears the words of God, "Be strong and courageous. Do not be frightened, and do not be dismayed, for the LORD your God is with you wherever you go" (Josh. 1:9). As he looked at the satanic visage and at the precipice below, he remembered what Israel had forgotten: "When you go out to war against your enemies, and see horses and chariots and an army larger than your own, you shall not be afraid of them, for the LORD your God is with you, who brought you up out of the land of Egypt" (Deut. 20:1).

Moreover, the invisibility of Jesus' protection was preparation for his kingship. The king of Israel, after all, was required not to return to Egypt to acquire horses (Deut. 17:16). Why not? It is because the Israelite king is to see his protection through the power of God, not by the same standards as the slavery from which his people have come. The king's power is to be through the Spirit, not by visible might and power.

Jesus' forefather David was tested at this point, also out in the wilderness. David, like Jesus, had been anointed the legitimate king. But, like Jesus, this was not yet publicly recognized. Since David bore the Spirit, he knew that God would grant him the power to fight his enemies. But his enemy was Saul, who currently held the office of Israelite ruler. As David was being chased by Saul's troops, a moment of testing came. David and his men were in a cave when they came upon Saul, who came in there to relieve his bowels. David's men saw this as a turn of events from the Lord. By pinning Saul to the ground with his spear—which would have been easy to do—David could protect himself from physical threat and could assume the kingdom. This would have verified for David which of the two "sons" God would stand with. David refused to strike and instead merely cut a square off Saul's robe—because he feared God more than he feared his enemy. David refused to put God to the test.

David's wisdom here did not hold in the years after he left the desert and ascended the throne. The shepherd-king jeopardized his kingship by ordering a census, a count of all Israel's men and armaments. This hardly sounds all that treacherous to us, especially those of us who live in countries that regularly conduct a census. But David was seeking out the numbers of a potential standing army. And this, in the words of one commentator, was to be "a kind of barometer of the Lord's favor."[3] But David shouldn't have needed a barometer. He had the Word of God. This test exposes a hidden flaw in David's heart, a craving for verifiable security apart from a faithful trust in God.

Jesus refused to force God's protection—by throwing himself from the pinnacle—because he already "saw" it by faith. Jesus saw through the Devil's implications, understanding that Psalm 91 does not teach that the anointed of God will not face trouble. The song says instead that the trouble will not triumph over the anointed. "You will tread on the lion and the adder," the Psalm says, "the young lion and the serpent you will trample underfoot" (v. 13). The Devil had heard this language before (Gen. 3:15). God did promise to protect his anointed, but not by exempting him from trouble. Instead the promise is that God would be "with him in trouble" (Ps. 91:15) by prompting him to call out to his Father. "Because he holds fast to me in love, I will deliver him," God announces in the Psalm. "I will protect him, because he knows my name" (Ps. 91:14).

Now, this temptation comes to all of us, though in different ways. For some the temptation hits at the most primal level of following Christ—assurance of faith. You might be one of those Christians who are constantly in fear that you're not "really saved." Now, of course, it could be that's the case, and what you're sensing is the conviction of God's Spirit pointing out that what you professed earlier wasn't genuine saving faith. My words to you would be simple: repent and believe the gospel. Many Christians, though, are trusting in Jesus and repenting of sin, but they still don't "feel" as though Jesus has received them. Usually what these tormented souls want is some kind of verification that they are really, really accepted by God. For some that is some sort of visible blessing. For others it's a kind of settled intuition of their personal salvation. For others it is some kind of measurable uptick in sanctification, which can be filed and referred back to when needed. For others it's some sort of miracle.

In contemporary Western evangelical life, some of this search for tangible security has shown up in the use of the so-called sinner's prayer. I do not want to be misunderstood as saying that the sinner's prayer is satanic. I first met Christ by praying a sinner's prayer ("Lord, have mercy on me, a sinner"), and I lead people to faith in Christ all the time by means of praying for God's forgiveness. The problem is not the prayer. The problem is that some Christians use the prayer as a mechanized way of bestowing some type of verifiable assurance. Many of us have prayed different versions of some kind of prefabricated evangelistic prayer dozens or even hundreds of times just in case we lacked the requisite "sincerity" the first few times around. Some preachers will even encourage crowds of Christians to pray the sinner's prayer again, to, as they put it, "nail it down." These Christians are told they can pray the sinner's prayer and have a card signed by the person praying and a witness of the moment they came to know Christ. "If you ever then doubt that you're a Christian," the preacher says, "you can just pull out that card and look at it."

Now that's obviously far from the freedom and simplicity of the gospel. Some more theologically-minded evangelicals denounce and ridicule these old revivalist practices with bravado. But they then fall into a similar trap as they languish in depression until they've worked through long checklists to see if they have maintained quantifiable "fruits" of conversion, questioning every thought and motive. This is not the way of faith.

Yes, faith requires a confession with the mouth of Jesus' lordship and a belief in the heart of his resurrection (Rom. 10:9–10). Yes, faith is obedient (James 2:14–26) and works itself out in love (Gal. 5:6). The problem isn't with either of these truths. The problem is that we want to find our security in something we can measure—a piece of paper, a remembered time of tears, the fact that by our calculations we're three times more humble than we were this time last year. The problem is that these things don't assure us either. The unsaved "goats" at the Judgment Seat have lists of reasons why they're assured of salvation, while the saved "sheep" seem comparatively silent (Matt. 7:22; 25:31–46).

Many of us, when we grapple with sin or when difficult times come into our lives, want to pull back the veil of the universe to see if God is really there. But faith isn't like that. Faith is believing something—such as that God accepts you in Christ Jesus—on the basis of his Word, not on the basis of what you can mark down and verify. Imagine for a moment that an angel appears to you and promises that you can know with certainty the existence of God, the truth of the gospel, and your eternal standing with Christ. All you have to do is jump from the highest point of the temple—God will catch you. I wonder how many of us, in the darkest nights of our soul, would take that plunge.

The temptation toward self-protection moves with us as we move forward in the Christian life. In our dialogue with those outside the faith, we often fall for this temptation not only in tone (as we'll see shortly) but also in content. We often want an incontrovertible, airtight argument for the truthfulness of the Christian gospel, something that can be tested and verified. We want to see Jesus—and thus ourselves—protected from any possible attack. Some do this by resting everything on intellectually rigorous arguments—historical evidence for the resurrection, say, or on the intricate structure of the human eye, or whatever. Others do this by looking for dramatic public evidences of God's existence—in miracles or healings or revivals. This is an old and persistent strain in Christian life. The apostle Paul wrote to the church at Corinth that the Greeks demanded signs of wisdom and the Jews demanded signs of power, but it was through the apostolic preaching that the aspirations of both were found in Christ, who is "the power of God and the wisdom of God" (1 Cor. 1:24). Humanly speaking, this was a paradoxically weak power and a paradoxically foolish wisdom. But Christ alone could illuminate and overcome the darkness out there and in here.

Sometimes believers will throw up their hands in frustration with non-Christian people they know. "I have said everything I know to say to her about the gospel," one might say. "She already knows it all and doesn't believe." Often what we seek is another argument, a hidden angle that our interlocutor hasn't thought through before. But that's rarely how the gospel is heard and received. Think about it in your own case. Did you believe the gospel the first time you ever heard it? Perhaps you did, but if so, you're quite unusual. Most of us heard the gospel over and over and over again until one day it hit us in a very different way. And what was different about it? Was it a new argument? Did you say to yourself, "Wait, you mean there's archaeological evidence proving the historical existence of the Hittites?" or "Hold on, there were five hundred witnesses to the resurrection? Well, what must I do to be saved?"

No, in most cases what we heard was the same old gospel—Christ crucified for us, buried, raised from the dead—and suddenly there was light (2 Cor. 4:6). Suddenly what had seemed boring or irrelevant to us now seemed quite personal. We heard a man's voice in that gospel, and we wanted to follow that voice (John 10:3, 16). We saw a light of glory that overwhelmed us (2 Cor. 4:6). The same is true with the as-of-yet unbelieving world around us or the as-of-yet unbelieving relatives we have waiting for us at the Thanksgiving dinner table. You need not be intimidated by unbelievers, as though what you need is a more nuanced "worldview" to protect the kingdom of God from their threats. Yes, we engage in apologetic arguments, but those aren't at the hub of our mission. By talking with unbelievers about arguments against the existence of God or scientific evidence for blind natural selection or whatever, all we're doing is listening to the defense mechanisms of those who are, as we were, scared of the sound of God's presence in the garden. We should talk about those things lovingly, but not so we can defend the faith. We engage others only so we can get to the only announcement that assaults the blinding power of the god of this age (2 Cor. 4:4). The gospel is big enough to fight for itself.

The temptation to self-protection also shows up often in the way we view God's blessing on us and the mystery of our future. Consider, for instance, the persistent issue, all over the world, of the scandal-ridden charlatan "faith healer." I'm not dubious about healing. I believe God heals, and often does so miraculously. And I believe God gifts some people to be especially efficacious in their prayers for the healing of others. But we all know there are those who will use the power of God to peddle a product, and the sick and desperate are a target market for such predators. I fear we have created a market for this phenomenon by our refusal to spend time praying for the healing of the sick among us.

Of course, all our churches have prayer lists for the sick, and many churches go over these lists line by line in the Wednesday night prayer meeting or in the home Bible study group. But let's be honest, aren't most of these "prayer requests" more akin to a news bulletin or a public service announcement? When is the last time you saw a church follow the command of the Holy Spirit as to what to do for the sick, as found in James 5:13–15? When is the last time you saw a disease-ravaged Christian call the elders of his church for anointing with oil and fervent prayer for healing? Perhaps if such were more commonplace, the wounded among us would have less reason to drive past our churches to seek out the self-appointed apostle in the carnival tent down the road.

Problematic even beyond that, though, is our insistence on seeing our health and well-being—our visible protection—as itself a sign of God's presence and love. This is precisely what Jesus refused to do from the tip of the temple. True, most of us are not the kind of "health, wealth, and prosperity gospel" teachers we see on the most garish outposts of crypto-Canaanite Christian television. But, truth be told, most of us are indeed "health, wealth, and prosperity gospel" adherents when it comes to what we expect for our own lives. Instead of humbly praying and seeking God's blessings, many of us bargain with God, expecting him to keep us protected as part of some cosmic arrangement.

Back in the sixteenth century, the Christian pastor-theologian John Calvin saw this as a common obstacle to authentic communion with God. Calvin identified the tendency to "tempt God" among those who "covenant with God only under certain conditions, and, as if he were the servant of their own appetites, bind him to laws of their own stipulation." Calvin continued, "If he does not obey them at once, they become indignant, grumble, protest, murmur, and rage at him."[4] Most of us wouldn't see ourselves in such a category. No one would until the kind of disappointment hits that would uncover such an attitude.

When our ultimate goal becomes security and protection, God becomes a means to that security and protection. We "test" him then, to see if he is able to serve as a means to our real god, our sense that everything will be all right. As long as we see our way toward physical, emotional, financial, relational, or familial well-being, God is welcome. But when such things are threatened, we indict God with our grumbling, even when we carefully disguise this as a "venting" against our circumstances, not against God. We assume that God's love entails God's visible protection *right now*. When that is absent, we grow distant and prayerless toward God. We put him to the test.

I heard not long ago from a man I haven't seen since high school. When asked about his religious beliefs, he simply says he is "an atheist until proven otherwise." I fear sometimes that despite all my Sunday learning I'm the same thing. It's not just that I want to be protected from whatever scares me—I want to be reassured now that this protection will always be there. I want Christ, but I too often want him as a kind of quantifiable spiritual asset, as something I can always check to be sure of just as I can check my bank account balance or my cholesterol level. I want what God has promised, but I want power of attorney to execute those promises when I determine I need them. That's not what the gospel of Jesus Christ is all about.

What ultimately undoes the pull to self-protection is the cross. Jesus refused to seek the proof of his own protection because he was seeking more than his own protection. He was looking for you, and you weren't on the pinnacle of the temple. You were outside the camp, cut off from the presence of God. Jesus didn't throw himself from the high place for the same reason that a faithful husband doesn't run out of a burning building to call a lawyer to sue the arsonist if he knows his wife is trapped inside. Jesus didn't come to protect himself. He came for the world. He came for the church. He came for you. He bore your reproach, strapped on your curse, carried your exile. This other-directedness freed Jesus to live out a very different life from the cringing, anxiety-filled lives so many of us carry on.

Satan moved on, of course, from this second temptation, but he would return with it. Jesus would hear it again from his own follower and friend Peter, who vowed to fight anyone who tried to take Jesus to crucifixion. Indeed, when the authorities came to arrest Jesus, Peter unsheathed his sword and lopped off the ear of one of the arresting officials. Jesus turned and rebuked his friend, pointing out exactly what he knew there on the pinnacle's point: "Do you think that I cannot appeal to my Father, and he will at once send me more than twelve legions of angels?" (Matt. 26:53). With the question of protecting self over against the cross, Jesus identified the spirit behind Peter's pugnacity—Satan himself (Matt. 16:23).

At first glance the second temptation might seem to be a temptation to engage in risky behavior. After all, what could be riskier than throwing yourself off a tower in hopes that some angels will catch you? But this action would have instead been an evasion of risk. Jesus could have in this way cleared away all the ambiguity and faced his enemies with the clear, proven truth that his Father was on his side. But it was Jesus' refusal to jump that was courageous. As the Spirit of Christ forms the kingdom and clears away the strongholds in your life, you'll find yourself drawn toward courage over against fearful self-protection as well.

My friend Patrick Henry Reardon notes that "courage" is an elusive virtue in the contemporary context. Because we imagine ourselves to need "safety" and "security" in every aspect of life (even sex!), we've lost something of the feel of what it means to learn faith through valor. "Meanwhile, bravery has been replaced by sheer stupidity," Reardon writes. "Examples of such replacement include things like skydiving and bungee jumping, which serve no purpose except the thrill of supposed danger. A largely illusory peril is cultivated for purely emotional purposes."[5]

Indeed, when genuine bravery is sacrificed to an ethic of self-protection, the result is not avoidance of risk but, as in the Devil's suggestion to Jesus, an embrace of meaningless risk. If, for example, one of the critical responsibilities of fatherhood is protection, then what happens to a society when fathers are often absent or neglectful or abusive? The result is not always a kind of cringing passivity in the next generation (although that's often part of it). The result is often a kind of hypermasculine predatory male. Unable to see the model of a self-sacrificial, self-risking kind of protective fatherhood, he replaces bravery with a kind of violent swagger. The Spirit of Christ, though, calls us to a different kind of security and a different kind of risk.

Hannah can hardly stand to look at old family pictures, seeing her parents smiling, with their arms around each other. She had respected her dad for his Christian conviction and his spiritual leadership, and she always said she wanted to marry someone just like him when she grew up. When Hannah was seventeen, she found out her father had been carrying on an affair with a woman not all that much older than she. Her parents divorced soon afterward, and nothing much was the same after that. Hannah is a little older now and is herself married, a newlywed. She is tormented by the thought that her new husband might one day do to her what her father did to her mother.

She is constantly interrogating her husband, jealous of any woman who even speaks to him. Despite the fact that her husband seems to love her and to be a man of integrity, Hannah can't help but think that her father seemed that way too. In some ways what Hannah is going through is just normal adjustment for someone who has been hurt badly. But in order for her to open herself up to love, she's going to have to accept that she will never be able to uproot any possibility of risk from her marriage. She's going to have to love even without "proof" that she'll never be hurt.

But risk is inherent in every kind of other-directed life. Marriage could result in infidelity. Having children means you may well experience the anguish of seeing one of those children killed in a car accident or shipped home in a casket from a foreign war or sentenced to life without parole in a federal penitentiary. Courage isn't protecting yourself in a cocoon from these possibilities. Courage is walking forward and embracing others in love even though you may suffer greatly in ways you could never imagine now. Jesus walked that way before you, and he walks that way now with you. That's the way of the cross.

A QUESTION OF VINDICATION

"Man, she is crazy. You are better off without her." Chances are, reader, you've either said or heard something like that (with perhaps some change of wording and gender reference) at some point in your life. After a romantic breakup, most people seek out their friends. And most people have friends who will reassure them that they're not to blame and the rejecting party is. That doesn't go away once the ups and downs of courtship are over. The one who's been fired seeks to hear the same kind of conversation about his supervisor. In fact, it doesn't even take a firing. There's a reason the most popular person around the office break room is the one who'll moderate a list of grievances against the boss. This gives a feeling of empowerment to people who want to show they're in the right after all.

There's something natural about all of that, despite how it is twisted into sinful ways. One of the core principles of the universe, after all, is justice. Part of justice is for things to be seen the way they are—for the heroes and the villains to be sorted out. In a Christian view of things, this primal sense of justice is because we were created with the hard-wired knowledge of Judgment Day, a day on which all the secrets will be exposed and the righteous publicly vindicated as such (Rom. 2:6–8). This public display of being in the right is called vindication, and it's a crucial aspect of something the Bible calls "glory."

Glory in biblical thought is the unapproachable, uncreated light that surrounds the triune God. Glory is also the fame and renown and acclaim of God. But glory also includes a theatrical component. It is the public display of God's goodness, truth, and beauty, and thus his praiseworthiness. One theologian defines God's glory as, in part, God's right to prove, declare, and "almost as it were to make himself conspicuous and everywhere apparent as the One he is."[6] Another notes that what it means for God to be glorified is that "each member of the Trinity speaks and acts in such a way as to enhance the reputations of the other two, to bring praise and honor to the other persons."[7] Created in the image of God, we long for the justice of the truth to be seen. Who are God's people? What is the right way to live? Who is in the right? We were shaped for glorification.

That public display of rightness is right at the core of what God has been doing in the world by protecting his people from evil. After all, God led his people Israel through the wilderness, protecting them from harm, in order to make for himself "a glorious name" (Isa. 63:14). God's people share in this vindication of God when he demonstrates their rightness among all the nations (Isa. 66:18; Ezek. 39:21). When God sets everything right in the end, then "the nations will know that I am the LORD who sanctifies Israel, when my sanctuary is in their midst forevermore" (Ezek. 37:28). Public vindication is a critical part of God's deliverance of his people. God doesn't simply set a table for me, the Scripture says; he sets this table "in the presence of my enemies" (Ps. 23:5).

The Devil's offer for Jesus to be delivered by angels is all about this. In Satan's scenario Jesus would have been not only protected, but protected before the audience of Jerusalem. He would have had not only the personal assurance of suspension of doom but also the celebrity prominence of a public deliverance. Remember Jesus' context here. Jesus was accused of being a slob, a drunk, an occultist. If he had thrown himself from the temple, these angelic warriors indeed would have rescued him. And all this would have happened in the most visible place possible, in the very epicenter of Israelite religion, politics, and commerce. It was, in fact, the place, the old prophecies said, to which the nations would stream to see the display of God's justice and glory.

All Jesus' claims about himself, about his Father, about his gospel would all have been seen to be true. After all, that's what's so persuasive about the Devil's speech. The Psalm he quotes promises, "With long life I will satisfy him and show him my salvation" (Ps. 91:16). There is in the biblical promise a very public repudiation of one's enemies and a very public affirmation of who it is that God considers to be on his side (Ps. 89:49–51). The shame that the anointed bears, the Scripture says, includes the insults that come from those who say, "When will he die, and his name perish?" (Ps. 41:5). The answer comes with the vindicating deliverance of God: "By this I know that you delight in me: my enemy will not shout in triumph over me" (Ps. 41:11). C. S. Lewis famously said that Jesus' claims about himself mean that he was "liar, lunatic, or Lord."[8] Jesus could have solved that trilemma incontrovertibly right there.

Again, Jesus is standing here in the middle of our stories. Part of God's deliverance of Israel from Egypt was, by protecting the Israelites from the plagues, putting forth a "sign" to Pharaoh distinguishing who God's people were (Ex. 8:23). God relented from destroying his people Israel in the wilderness because Moses pleaded with his God to think of the sign that such judgment would send to their enemies: "Why should the Egyptians say, 'With evil intent did he bring them out, to kill them in the mountains and to consume them from the face of the earth'?" (Ex. 32:12).

The vindication of God was essential also to the story of Jesus' kingship. There is a reason, after all, that old King Saul was incensed when the crowds began singing, "Saul has struck down his thousands, and David his ten thousands" (1 Sam. 18:7–8). Saul grumbled with jealousy, "And what more can he have but the kingdom?" (v. 8). When Saul began to come after David to destroy him, Saul's son pointed to David's deliverance from enemies as a sign of God's favor: "For he took his life in his hand and he struck down the Philistine, and the LORD worked a great salvation for all Israel. You saw it, and rejoiced. Why then will you sin against innocent blood by killing David without cause?" (1 Sam. 19:5). That deliverance from the hand of Goliath—and earlier "from the paw of the lion and from the paw of the bear" (1 Sam. 17:37)—was about more than physical safety alone. It was indeed about more than David's seeing that God was on his side. The scavenging birds and animals eating the skin from the corpse of the Philistine warrior happened so "that all the earth may know that there is a God in Israel, and that all this assembly may know that the LORD saves not with sword and spear. For the battle is the LORD's, and he will give you into our hand" (1 Sam. 17:46–47). God's protection from harm was a demonstration of the fact that he was fighting for his chosen king. A king defeated in battle evidenced a loss of blessing—and possibly a loss of anointing—from the Lord. Jesus could have proven he was the son of his Father, to himself and to the watching Jerusalem, in the time it takes to jump off a ledge.

Jesus knew, though, that self-directed vindication is no vindication at all. The man and the woman, after all, tried to prove their rightness after their rebellion (Gen. 3:12–13). The Israelites, caught in their manifold idolatries, continually sought publicly to prove their rightness, even to God. Aaron, the golden calf-maker, even went so far as to suggest that he had simply thrown the earrings into the fire "and out came this calf" (Ex. 32:24). Saul's loss of the kingship came partly through his increasingly desperate attempts to vindicate himself as the true anointed of God in the eyes of his people.

And perhaps as Jesus gazed out over the land of God's promise, he also thought of one body that couldn't be found there— that of Moses. The Israelites' "test" at Massah, after all, wasn't the end of the matter. At Meribah the people grumbled once again because of a lack of water. God directed Moses once again to the life-giving rock. He instructed his prophet to "tell the rock before their eyes to yield its water" (Num. 20:8). But Moses did something a bit different. Instead, Moses did what God had demanded in another context, not in this one. He struck the rock with his staff as he yelled, "Hear now, you rebels: shall we bring water for you out of this rock?" (Num. 20:10). God gave the water, just as he had promised, but he said to Moses, "Because you did not believe in me, to uphold me as holy in the eyes of the people of Israel, therefore you shall not bring this assembly into the land that I have given them" (Num. 20:12).

That seems kind of capricious, doesn't it? Why would God keep a faithful, humble leader from the land he'd traveled forty years to see because of one instant's motion of a stick against a stone? There are, I think, several reasons here, but one of them is that Moses exchanged his role of deliverer for an opportunity for self-vindication. Rather than speaking to the rock, he spoke to the crowds, expressing his outrage, protecting his leadership, vindicating his own name. God said that momentary action disinherited the leader of God's people from finding rest in the fulfillment of God's promise. A stick and a stone—and some words—cost Moses his inheritance. Jesus would not make the same error.

Jesus didn't test God to prove himself to be in the right, because Jesus understood the fatherhood of God. Public vindication is part of God's fatherly protection of his Son.

Jesus had heard the voice that declared, "You are my beloved

Son." He knew based on the Word of God that he is who God says he is. And he will not obey a satanic desire to be proven and to be seen to be right in the here and now. We, like Jesus, want to be protected from harm, and we want to be seen to be right. When this is abstracted from Judgment Day, though, and made into a commodity that God owes us, it grows malignant and demonic.

Think, for instance, about the way you receive personal criticism. For some of us, even the mildest suggestion that someone might not like us becomes an opportunity for a full-fledged campaign to prove that we're in the right. Aaron and Naomi are a young Christian couple. Both come from nominally Christian families that long ago stopped taking spiritual things seriously. They don't understand why these two are so committed to religion. This especially shows up in the raising of children. Aaron and Naomi believe children to be a blessing from the Lord, and while their family is not large in comparison to families in other places and times, their four young children seem to be a burdensomely enormous family to some, especially to Naomi's mother. Naomi hears from her extended family things along the lines of "Wow, you have your hands full" and "Whew, I wouldn't want to trade places with you." Naomi's mother will occasionally make comments about how she's afraid her daughter who is "smart enough to do anything" is now "wasting" her life as "just a mom."

Both Aaron and Naomi find themselves on edge around their parents, and they have started to recognize that disciplining their children is much harder at this time. It dawned on them one day that what they were disciplining wasn't disobedience but the appearance of "chaos." They didn't want to give their families "evidence" that they were "overwhelmed." They knew their children were a blessing, and they wanted to prove it by having everything organized just so. What they wanted was vindication, to be proven right in front of their skeptical parents' eyes. They wanted to win the argument.

I am part of a very conservative Protestant denomination

of churches, a denomination that underwent no small trauma a generation ago over issues of biblical orthodoxy. I happen to agree with the conservatives that the Scripture is without error, that faith in Christ is necessary for salvation, and other such matters. A decade ago, when I was a young seminary student, I was asked by our denominational news service to cover the national general assembly of the more liberal dissident group within our denomination. No one knew me there, so I had free rein to walk around the exhibit hall, talk to leaders of the group, and read the materials being handed out. Some of these leaders, and some of these written materials, held to some views on issues quite out of the mainstream for our "tribe" (though fairly typical within mainline Protestantism of the time). I wrote a series of articles "exposing" these views and implicitly accusing the leadership of this group of a biblically unfaithful kind of radicalism.

Everything I'd written had been accurate. The more "progressive" wing of the group—the ones lobbying for a faster move in a different direction—were actually the kindest to me since we both understood the stakes but simply disagreed about whether they could be part of a biblically faithful Christianity. But I came under intense criticism from the organization. They accused me of sensationalizing the situation for "political" purposes. Some of them approached me after the stories started to be published during the gathering to let me know exactly what they thought of me and my "ilk." That's when it became, for me, a crusade, a crusade very dangerous for my soul. As it started to become more and more evident that the issues I'd uncovered were, in fact, a real point of tension in the group rather than just something on the extreme fringe, I gloried in being proved right.

Again, the issues were important. And I believe we need a free press willing to inform people about such goings-on rather than allowing leaders (of either Right or Left) to cover over decision-making processes. But even in my zeal to do what was right, I had become more devilish than Christian in how

I carried it out. I was protecting myself, vindicating myself. The truth of God's Scripture wasn't what was motivating me. Even on the issues on which I was right, the issues had simply become an extension of myself. I wasn't fighting for Christ or for his Church. I was fighting for my own honor, my own self-image, my own reputation. What I thought was conviction was actually bloodlust. Some of the people I opposed had ideas that really were wrongheaded, but their concept of my accusatory muckraking grew to be more and more true. They may or may not have been wrong about Jesus and wrong about Scripture, but they were certainly right about me.

Chances are, you probably won't ever have to face your "opponents," real or imagined, on the other side of a press pass, but you will consistently face the pull to direct your own vindication. Maybe you look at your old workplace, the one that mistreated you, and take a secret thrill at watching their profits decline. Maybe you think about that teacher who told you you'd never make it, and part of your success now is a way of saying, "How do you like me now?" Maybe you enjoy telling about the fracturing marriage of the spouse who left you years ago. "What goes around comes around," you say to your friends.

Moreover, there is a real danger of a self-vindicating, self-protecting kind of mentality showing up even in the way we as Christian churches speak to and about the unbelievers in our communities and neighborhoods. As I write these words right now, I'm sitting in a coffee shop in my community. Outside my window there are two cars, one brandishing a bumper magnet of a "Darwin fish," the early Christian emblem of the fish, growing legs with the word "Darwin" inside. Next to it is a car, I'm guessing owned by a Christian, with a bumper sticker of that Darwin fish being devoured by a larger Jesus fish. Is this really an evangelistic tool?

Has there ever been an atheistic evolutionist who has seen such a thing and concluded, "You know, Darwinism is crazy. Where can I find a gospel tract to show me how to believe?" I doubt it. Instead, much of our rhetoric is less about persuading unbelievers, or maintaining the faith of believers, than about, as Thomas Merton put it a generation ago, our search for "an argument strong enough to prove us 'right.'"[9] That's why we caricature the views of our opponents in a way that can get loud "amens" in our own settings but leave our children completely unprepared for the more careful, nuanced arguments they find when they actually encounter the viewpoints we've lampooned.

What is the end result? The end result is a self-referential Christian rhetoric that not only fails to persuade outsiders but also fails to protect our own children and grandchildren from what we're afraid of exposing them to in the first place. That leaves us with what amounts to, in the words of one secularist critic, little more than "a perpetual outrage machine."[10] In fact, our overheated "culture war" rhetoric represents the pitiful sound and fury of what William Faulkner once called "an enraged impotence."[11]

This doesn't mean we shouldn't confront culture. Jesus, the prophets before him, and the apostles after him all did so. If we are, as Jesus said, "fishers of men" (Matt. 4:19), then we understand that the ecosystem in which the fish live matters. But we must confront culture with a certain kind of willingness to be, as Paul said to the church at Corinth, "wronged" and "defrauded" (1 Cor. 6:7), knowing our ultimate vindication comes later. We need not respond back to unbelievers in kind with sarcastic barbs and slickly packaged campaigns to protect our "right" to be free from ridicule.

We ought to be willing to be ridiculed and scoffed at because our audience isn't this present band of spectators. We can listen to them, love them, and bear their arguments with the same patience with which we comfort our children when they insist to us there's a goblin under the bed. I know there's no goblin. And I know Darwinism and hedonism and nihilism and whatever else is the proposed alternative to a Christian vision of things aren't true. Sure, I'll open the window and show my son that what he hears is just a dead leaf banging against the window screen. And I'll show my non-Christian neighbor how not even he believes the universe is random and meaningless and amoral. But I don't rage against my little son's "stupidity" in crying about the goblin. He's a child. And I don't rage against my unbelieving neighbor's unbelief. He's held captive to a mind-blinding snake (2 Cor. 4:3–4). In both cases, what's important is something other than that I'm proven to be right. What's important is truth and hope and, above all these, love.

Jesus knew Israel's quarreling with God at the wilderness waterside was just the beginning. That water-bearing rock, after all, wasn't just an inanimate thing. Somehow, mystically, the Scripture tells us, "the Rock was Christ" (1 Cor. 10:4). Once again, as at the bitter waters, God's people were put to the test. And once again they thought they were the ones doing the testing. They charged Jesus with being a threat—to the religious order and to the political empire. And believing themselves to be doing the will of God, they hanged him, in accordance with the Scriptures, as a blasphemer outside the camp (Deut. 21:22–23). If they had but spoken to the rock, God would have given them living water to drink. Instead those in Moses' seat sought to vindicate their own rightness, and they struck the rock. Surely no one thought about Meribah when they saw a Roman pulling a spear out of his abdomen as water gushed to the ground below.

Part of the curse Jesus would bear for us on Golgotha was the taunting and testing by God's enemies. As he drowned in his own blood, the spectators yelled words quite similar to those of Satan in the desert: "Let the Christ, the King of Israel, come down now from the cross that we may see and believe" (Mark 15:32). But he didn't jump down. He didn't ascend to the skies. He just writhed there. And, after it all, the bloated corpse of Jesus hit the ground as he was pulled off the stake, spattering warm blood and water on the faces of the crowd.

That night the religious leaders probably read Deuteronomy 21 to their families, warning them about the curse of God on those who are "hanged on a tree." Fathers probably told their sons, "Watch out that you don't ever wind up like him." Those

Roman soldiers probably went home and washed the blood of Jesus from under their fingernails and played with their children in front of the fire before dozing off. This was just one more insurrectionist they had pulled off a cross, one in a line of them dotting the roadside. And this one (what was his name? Joshua?) was just decaying meat now, no threat to the empire at all.

That corpse of Jesus just lay there in the silence of that cave. By all appearances it had been tested and tried, and found wanting. If you'd been there to pull open his bruised eyelids, matted together with mottled blood, you would have looked into blank holes. If you'd lifted his arm, you would have felt no resistance. You would have heard only the thud as it hit the table when you let it go. You might have walked away from that morbid scene muttering to yourself, "The wages of sin is death."

But sometime before dawn on a Sunday morning, a spike-torn hand twitched. A blood-crusted eyelid opened. The breath of God came blowing into that cave, and a new creation flashed into reality. God was not simply delivering Jesus—and with him all of us—from death, he was also vindicating him—and with him all of us. By resurrecting Jesus from the dead, God was reaffirming what he had said over the Jordan waters. He was declaring Jesus "to be the Son of God in power" (Rom. 1:4). This was done, that Scripture says, by "the Spirit of holiness." This is the same Spirit who rested on Jesus at his baptism "like a dove" (Matt. 3:16). As this dovish Spirit alighted on him in the water and in the tomb, could Jesus have thought of the words of the Psalm the Devil would quote in the wilderness: "He will cover you with his pinions, and under his wings you will find refuge" (Ps. 91:4)? With that kind of rescue, who needs to be proven right in any other way?

CONCLUSION

The Devil was right, you know. Jesus refused to heed his offer not because the tempter was wrong but precisely because he was quoting an accurate Scripture. God indeed would rescue his anointed. But the anointed is the one who waits on God and who refuses to force his hand. We must suffer with Christ before we are glorified with him (Rom. 8:17). To seek a "security" apart from Christ, a vindication apart from Christ, is to taunt God by asking, "Is the Lord among us or not?"

We don't need to protect our lives because our lives are already crucified. We are, the gospel tells us, "hidden with Christ in God" (Col. 3:3). We can know then, whatever comes at us, "When Christ who is your life appears, then you also will appear with him in glory" (Col. 3:4). We can be willing then to lose our lives, our reputations, and our arguments because we can't hold on to anything by our cunning strategies anyway. In the long run we're all dead, and in the longer run we're all raised from the dead. There's a freedom that comes from seeing that.

Jesus knew that God's protection was better than self-protection. He knew that God's vindication was better than self-vindication. He had time to wait to be rescued, time to wait to be right. That time was in the Easter tomb and then in the eastern skies. He was willing to trust God's Word and to be seen to be wrong in the meantime.

After I pulled off my noise-canceling earphones and slinked back in my chair on the plane flight, I eventually stopped blushing. But the more I thought about it, the more convicted I became about why I'd been so enthusiastic in that moment with my singing. I was singing with far more gusto than I do, typically, when I'm gathered with God's people in worship. The more I think about it, the more I realize that my freedom in that moment was because I'd forgotten myself. I wasn't worried about what anyone thought or even about my own conception of myself. I was free.

The satanic powers always want us to question that freedom, to pull us back to the slavery of "security." What changes all that is what the Spirit showed Jesus from the temple's tip—the protecting, accepting fatherhood of God. I don't need to "test" God's view of me. I don't need to protect myself or vindicate myself. I sure don't need to hide. If the Word of God is true, then God sees me in Christ Jesus, and I have then already been executed, buried, and raised from the dead. I am safe.

All my self-protection is pathetic because it obscures the most important truth I've ever known—the gospel. How can I fear death when I've already drowned in my own blood, already been spiked to a pole in the Middle East? How can I fear public humiliation when I've already been dressed up in a king costume in order to be tortured by my country's occupiers? All that has happened to me because I am in Christ. His life is my life. And not only that, but God has already proven to me what he thinks of me. No satanic scaremongering can overcome what God has proclaimed:

> Sing aloud, O daughter of Zion;
>> shout, O Israel!
> Rejoice and exult with all your heart,
>> O daughter of Jerusalem!
> The LORD has taken away the judgments against you;
>> he has cleared away your enemies.
> The King of Israel, the LORD, is in your midst;
>> you shall never again fear evil.
> On that day it shall be said to Jerusalem:
> "Fear not, O Zion;
>> let not your hands grow weak.
> The LORD your God is in your midst,
>> a mighty one who will save;
> he will rejoice over you with gladness;
>> he will quiet you by his love;
> he will exult over you with loud singing.
> I will gather those of you who mourn for the festival,
>> so that you will no longer suffer reproach.
> Behold, at that time I will deal
>> with all your oppressors.
> And I will save the lame
>> and gather the outcast,
> and I will change their shame into praise
>> and renown in all the earth.

At that time I will bring you in,
    at the time when I gather you together;
for I will make you renowned and praised
    among all the peoples of the earth,
when I restore your fortunes
    before your eyes," says the LORD. (Zeph. 3:14–20)

So reject the voice pushing you to the death spiral, and don't be afraid. Why do you care what your supporters or your critics think of you? Why do you fear whatever it is that's scaring you? Look out over that ledge, and sing out to your Father. Sing loudly. Sing with the freedom of the already rescued, with the freedom of a people who have nothing to prove. And, as you sing, remember: he's singing back.

5

DESERT REIGN

Why We'd Rather Be Magnified Than Crucified

I guess it's hard enough to raise your children right without having to send them off to a Satanist every weekend. That was the dilemma a group of women had when they filed suit against the one thing they all had in common with each other—an ex-husband named Jamie. Jamie was a thirty-year-old factory worker, and he'd led a rough life. Then he wound up in court trying to convince a judge he was fit to have parental custody of his children. It all came down to a tattoo.

Jamie had a cross on his arm, embedded in ink in his skin. That might not seem all that controversial, except that the cross was upside down. And it formed the "t" in the word "Satan." Jamie's attorney said this was a simple religious liberty issue. He was a member of the Church of Satan and shouldn't be discriminated against because of his beliefs. The Devil's advocate called a satanic priest as an expert witness to provide the crux of their argument: satanism doesn't have anything to do with the Devil. The satanist said that their religion doesn't believe in a real, personal devil or in any god or supernatural power. Satanism instead worships the ego, the power of the self. That's what the upside-down cross is about, the turning on its head of the Christian values of humility, meekness, and servitude. Satanism isn't really devil worship, he said, since Satan is just a symbol for "pride, liberty, and individualism."[1]

Now, as I'm sure you can already tell from reading this far in this book, I disagree with the occultist about the existence of Satan. But let's give the Devil his due. It would be hard to find a more biblical definition of devil worship than the worship of pride, liberty, and individualism. As I read about somebody like Jamie, I'm always curious as to what happened in his life. After all, devil worship, like all forms of occultism, tends to show up, after a series of dark and dreadful steps, in the life of someone with almost nothing left to lose. Powerless people tend to be drawn to the occult, whether that's the pimpled teenage boy reading sorcery books to fend off the bullies or the middle-aged divorcée who finds self-confidence in her New Age earth religion or the coven of cultists drinking each other's blood. Those who have been hurt and marginalized can be drawn to the consolation of dark magic. For the rest of us, though, our quest for power tends to accept a subtler shade of Satanism.

I'm prideful, and so are you. Some of those who are reading this (maybe my grandmother) are probably mouthing the words, "Oh, he's not prideful at all. He's so sweet." That's just it, though. Many prideful people are so prideful they don't seem proud. We are disgusted enough by arrogance to want never to seem like the peacock poseurs we all have in our lives. But every human being bears the sinful tendency toward pride and exaltation of self. We express it in different ways, but we all crave power for ourselves and the freedom that seems to come with it. That's why Jesus went into the desert for us, to wrestle with our common temptation to worship the satanic world system around us.

In the climax of his wilderness temptations, Jesus found himself atop a high mountain. From here Satan showed him "all the kingdoms of the world and their glory" (Matt. 4:8). He told Jesus, "To you I will give all this authority and their glory, for it has been delivered to me, and I give it to whom I will" (Luke 4:6). All the power in the cosmos came with one condition and one condition only: "Fall down and worship me" (Matt. 4:9).

Jesus, again, didn't fall. He stood there, looked into the eyes of our demonic overlord, and quoted the Bible. Jesus went again to the words of Deuteronomy, paraphrasing God's command through Moses: "You shall worship the Lord your God and him only shall you serve" (Matt. 4:10). Jesus, resting in the fatherhood of God, knew that his inheritance, his kingdom, would come. He knew that God would exalt him; so he was able to humble himself before the mystery of God's mission. Jesus also mouthed the words that repelled the demon from his presence: "Be gone, Satan!" And Satan was gone.

If we follow Christ, we'll join this clash of the kingdoms too. You and I must discover what it is that people like us find so attractive about this Faustian exchange—worship and adoration for power and glory. We must see why we want to exchange the end-time exaltation by our Father for the right now exaltation of a snake. We must comprehend why we'd rather be magnified apart from Christ than crucified with him. That's a difficult concept for recovering satanists like us.

A QUESTION OF WISDOM

In every temptation the Devil ratcheted upward the imaginative lure of the offer. In the first he simply mentioned the bread, and in the second he took Jesus to the locale of a possible jump. In the third temptation, though, he actually showed Jesus the potential end result of the transaction. The unclean spirit took the Nazarene up on "a very high mountain," the Bible tells us. From there Jesus could see "all the kingdoms of the world and their glory" (Matt. 4:8).

Remember that Jesus was seeing all of this, almost certainly, for the very first time. That seems a strange concept to those who think of Jesus Christ as the ultimate cosmopolitan, a kind of detached citizen of everywhere and of nowhere. But seeing Jesus as the kind of generic, rootless, homogenized individual our contemporary society often mainstreams misses a central truth of the incarnation. Jesus is from somewhere. Jesus has a tribe—the people of Judah. He has a geographic background—he was from a little village in the Middle East. He has an accent—a northern Galilean one. And here this small-town laborer was seeing all the power in the world. This vision came with a startling simultaneity; it was all "in a moment of time" (Luke 4:5).

Maybe you, like Jesus, grew up in an isolated rural hamlet. Think of the first time you ever saw a place such as New York City or Paris or Tokyo, if you have. Wasn't it a dizzying experience to look up at the skyline above you? Or maybe you grew up instead in a cramped, noisy urban environment. Think of the first time you ever saw the Rocky Mountains or the Pacific Ocean or the Mojave Desert. Maybe your mouth stood agape just at the sight of the expanse of stars above you, stars that had been obscured by the electric lights or pollution that you took to be just part of the way things are. Now in reality, even these experiences wouldn't match what it would be like for a first-century Israelite to see this blast of worldly power and glory. After all, even before you saw the most awe-inspiring landscape you'd ever seen, you'd probably already seen it as some electronic image.

Now Jesus, of course, knew that he was the heir of God's kingdom. He would announce that (to much local consternation) shortly thereafter in his home synagogue. He knew from the Scriptures that God had promised "the ends of the earth" (Ps. 2:8) to him as an inheritance. But Jesus had received all of this by word, not by vision; by faith, not by sight. What God had veiled in future promise, Satan sought to uncover in present observation.

This is no new strategy. In every age Satan seeks to put us out of our mystery. With Eve, after all, the snake demystified the forbidden fruit and offered a picture of what her future would look like after her "liberation." She would be "like God, knowing good and evil" (Gen. 3:5). The people of Israel were led to clamor for a visible god to "go before us" (Ex. 32:1), a calf of gold they could see and touch. When King Saul was faced with the uncertainty of military victory or defeat, he was led to place his kingdom above waiting for the word of the Lord, and so he sought out a witch's séance to give him a vision of the future (1 Sam. 28:1–25). His power and glory were so precious to him that he chose to walk into occultism rather than to stand in ignorance.

The knowledge is important here because from the very beginning "the knowledge of good and evil" (Gen. 2:9, 17) has been a critical aspect of governing. Perhaps God eventually would have given Eve and her consort access to that forbidden tree, when they had been brought to the maturity needed to use it at God's direction. Adam and Eve were to be as little children, dependent on their Father even for the knowledge needed to gain their kingdom. David's son Solomon saw this, and God commends him in the pages of Scripture. Solomon confessed he was but a little child, that he didn't yet know good from evil (1 Kings 3:3–9). Rather than asking for power or wealth or kingdoms or glory for himself, he asked for wisdom. So God gave him the wisdom, and the kingdoms and the glory along with it (1 Kings 3:10–13). Later in the biblical story we find why this is so important. Wisdom isn't a self-directed intellect. Wisdom is a person—Christ, the wisdom of God and the power of God (1 Cor. 1:24). When Solomon sought wisdom, he was seeking Christ. When the Queen of Sheba "tested" Solomon with questions (1 Kings 10:1), she was testing the Spirit of Christ upon him. Centuries later Jesus would announce, "something greater than Solomon is here" (Matt. 12:42).

Satan was propping himself up as the vehicle of revelation. In explaining the purpose of the trees to Eve, he aped God's voice. In leading the Israelites to sacrifice to his demons, he parodied God's Word. Now he does the same thing by taking Jesus to the place where God would most famously unveil revelation—to a high mountain—to offer some disclosure of his own.

This is essential to Satan's core root of rebellion—pride. In his own story of downfall, the insurrectionist angel prized his knowledge that led to his wealth that led to his power that led to his exile (Ezek. 28:2–3). Since that time he is continually offering the power that comes along with knowledge, especially knowledge of the unknown future, and especially by fostering the kind of hubris that believes there are no limits to creaturely knowledge. It is no accident that immediately after Jesus' resurrection, the church was split apart by claims of secret knowledge as congregations ruptured into quarrels over genealogies and myths (1 Tim. 1:4; 2 John 7). The Devil knows, from personal experience, that knowledge "puffs up" (1 Cor. 8:1). Once you see what you could have, you can be turned toward craving it to the extent that you'll do whatever it takes to get it. "The lust of the eyes" incites "the pride of life" (1 John 2:16 KJV).

As Jesus' march to the kingdom unfolds in the Gospels, we are shown Jesus growing in wisdom and in knowledge (Luke 2:52). God was preparing his human nature to assume Adam's throne. As we grow up into Christ (Eph. 4:13–16), we follow the same path. We receive knowledge (Col. 2:2–3), but it is a knowledge that comes from God, a knowledge that is fit for a king or queen in training, for this particular moment in the training process, but not, as with God, a knowledge that is boundless. We learn to love both God's light-giving revelation and the limits of our ignorance, loving and trusting him even when we see "through a glass, darkly" (1 Cor. 13:12 KJV).

A satanic system of knowledge, though, eschews limits. Ignorance of any kind implies a finitude to humanity and, beyond that, a worship of another greater Source of wisdom and knowledge and the mysteries of life. The techno-utopian scientific era we live in is especially perilous in this regard. We demand an explanation for everything and a technological fix for every problem. But the wielding of data without wisdom can result not in the deification but the demonization of man.

Perhaps even more deadly, however, is a satanic use of knowledge in the interests of Christian theism. There's a kind of power that comes with an oversystematization of the beliefs of Christianity. You can learn to answer all the questions and provide tidy talking points to thorny problems, but you eventually lose reverence for and awe of God. You can wind up with a perfectly logical Aristotelian deity, or a self-reflecting Islamic deity, while losing sight of the paradoxical, mysterious, incomprehensible whirlwind of a Trinitarian God revealed to us in Jesus Christ. I suppose I recognized several years ago how far I had gone down this path when, in my reading of Scripture, I found a passage I'd never noticed before, and I was thrilled to find it. The verse was a perfect argument-ending volley I could send up in an ongoing theological debate I was having with a friend. After my minute or so of "eureka," I realized that the verse was a quote in the book of Job from Bildad the Shuhite, counsel God would later uproot as he commanded Job simply to shut his mouth before the mystery of God's sovereignty and goodness.

For most of us, the drive toward satanic knowledge won't be in the area of genetic manipulation or systematic theology. For most of us it will come in the drive to peer around the corner and see how everything will turn out. In order to grasp the little kingdom we want for ourselves, we toss about wondering what will happen next with our jobs, our health, our families, or our relationships. The satanic powers would offer to help us discover all of that. But in God's ordering of the universe, ignorance is often a blessing.

Just a few minutes ago, while I was writing this, a young couple whom I'd married to each other just over a year ago stopped by to talk. They have a newborn baby now and are nestling into life together in their first little apartment. Would they be better off knowing how successful he'll be in his career? Would it be good for them to know now about, God forbid, losing a daughter to leukemia or about the dementia one of them will get fifty years from now? Would they be more loved by God if they knew they would have financial security in twenty-five years or that their third son won't be able to keep a job? Most of us would love to know such things in advance if we could. But God knows better than we that we flourish as human beings when we learn, often through baby steps, to trust a Father's wisdom.

God revealed the mystery of Christ step-by-step, concealing the fullness of the revelation until the time was right (Rom. 16:25–26; Gal. 4:4; Eph. 3:5; Heb. 1:1–2; 1 Pet. 1:10–12). He does the same thing with each of our lives, promising us a goal of Christ-conformity and blessing, but asking us to walk toward it on the basis of "the assurance of things hoped for, the conviction of things not seen" (Heb. 11:1). Satan sought to present to Jesus his kingdom, as though he were the one with the right to unveil this glory, to disclose this mystery. The dark prince will do the same for you, and he'll convince you that your inability to see what's on the other side of the mountain for you is because God is holding you down. The moment you start to listen, to peer around the corner, you've started searching for another god.

A QUESTION OF WORSHIP

After showing Jesus the panorama of kingdoms, Satan offered them to him. All Jesus needed to do was to fall down in an instant of worship. As we've noted before, most people recognize devil worship as something wrong. Even the most nonreligious pluralist would have second thoughts about knowing her child's teacher was a Satanist. It seems so obviously twisted. That's why Jamie the tattoo-wearer had so many strikes against him going into court.

But if we're honest, we'll have to admit that for most people, worship seems to be something peripheral to life. Some are more honest about that than others. Humorist Florence King, for instance, speaks of her Anglo-Catholic worship as strictly a "genetic" thing. She is High Church because her people are, she writes, and she will "go to bat for transubstantiation, even though it means nothing to me one way or the other."[2] As one who lived among a congregation that could tolerate an openly adulterous worship leader but not one who didn't draw out the syllables in the chorus of "Count Your Many Blessings" properly, I can see something of how that happens, High Church,

Low Church, or anywhere in between. Both Jesus and Satan, though, knew better. Worship isn't simply about the singing of songs or the reading of prayers. Worship is the ascribing of worth, of value. Every act, every affection, every inclination then flows from whatever it is that we see and feel as ultimate. As Jesus and Satan looked out over those kingdoms, they both knew the hub of it all was worship.

In this offer Satan demonstrates the hubris that had brought him down from the heavenly places in the first place. Beyond the vision of the kingdoms, Satan models for Jesus what Jesus's own future could be like. The Devil boasts of all that authority and all that glory: "It has been delivered to me, and I give it to whom I will" (Luke 4:6). There's a sense of implied liberation and freedom in that statement. Satan sees himself as an autonomous agent, accountable to no one, with a power that is grounded simply in his own will.

Satan showed here explicitly what he'd been trying to do all along. Satan was not just trying to tempt Jesus; he was attempting to adopt Jesus. Satan, in all three temptations, is assuming the role of a father—first in provision, then in protection, and now in the granting of an inheritance. Satan didn't just want to be Jesus' lord; he wanted to be his father.

Spending so much of my time teaching churches about the biblical doctrine of adoption as it relates to orphan care, I'm realizing more and more that one reason few of us grasp the weight of our adoption in Christ is because so much of that truth rests on an understanding of inheritance. Few of us in the Western world these days really get the idea of inheritance because for us the concept seems to be a matter of "wealth management" for the most aristocratic enclaves of old money. For most of us, inheritance really isn't that big of a deal beyond writing out a will that tells our kids who gets Aunt Flossie's antique lampshade collection.

In the world of the Bible, though, the poor and working classes were the ones with the most at stake in the inheritance structure. There was no social welfare safety net, no collective retirement plan. The inheritance was the basic engine of family solidarity and economic survival. Your father worked not only to provide his children with the basic needs for living, but also to hand over that living and that occupation to those children when they were ready for it. His farmland or fishing boat or carpenter's tools would be his children's one day. You would work your whole life and hand something down to your own children too.

I say that we don't understand this concept, but in a very real sense most of us actually do. Many Christians—and I'm one of them—have been very critical of the tendency to confuse the kingdom of God with the "American Dream." Insofar as the American Dream is defined as more shopping and more consumption, the critique stands (see the first temptation). But, at least originally, the idea of the American Dream wasn't consumerist at all. It was instead the notion that anyone, without regard to nation of birth or social class or caste, could work hard, play by the rules, and make a better future for his or her family. The central thrust of this dream was that your children could be better off than you are. That's other directed and future oriented, not selfish. And it's not uniquely American. Almost every culture in the world includes parents who aspire to see that their children exceed them in education, opportunity, and prosperity. That's the reason the immigrant sanitation worker saves up to send her child to college. There's something heroic about that. Behind that impulse is the basic idea of inheritance, sacrificing yourself so you can lift up those who come after you.

This inheritance structure isn't merely a human cultural construct, designed to manage economic resources. It's rooted in the very order of the universe. Included in the image of God borne by our first parents, after all, was the promise that they were to work to protect the earth because it was all given to them. They were the heirs of the cosmos. Under God, theirs was the kingdom and the power and the glory, forever. The children of Abraham were likewise, by faith, inheritors of the land of Canaan and, ultimately, heirs of the world itself (Rom. 4:13).

This cosmic inheritance structure is why this was a real temptation, not just an act of theater. Jesus really wanted the kingdoms of the world and their glory. Jesus is the Son of God. He shares a nature with his Father and delights in what makes his Father happy (John 5:30). God is a happy ruler over everything that is. See his jubilation in the Psalms as they sing of the rule of God (e.g., Ps. 47; 50:1–2; 104; 111). God is the rightful king over this cosmos, and he loves it.

Moreover, Jesus as an unfallen human shares with us a nature designed for kingship. He was, after all, the "Christ," literally the one anointed to be king. Among the first words his mother heard about him, when confronted by an angel in Nazareth, was that he was to be the governor over Israel and the whole universe and that his kingdom would have no end (Luke 1:32–33). It is good for the kingdoms of this world to become the kingdoms of our Lord and of his Christ (Rev. 11:15). In fact, that's what all of history has been waiting for (Isa. 60:1–11; Eph. 1:10).

Satan pretended to be the keeper of this inheritance. He mimicked the humiliation-before-exaltation structure God had woven into the fabric of the cosmos. "Humble yourself before me," he suggested, "and I'll exalt you in due time." "To you I will give all this authority and their glory," the Devil said, "for it has been delivered to me, and I give it to whom I will" (Luke 4:6).

Once again the vain old dragon gloried in his own vanity, theatrically using language used by God himself about God himself: "The Most High God rules the kingdom of mankind and sets over it whom he will" (Dan. 5:21). Again the Devil's words were partly true. Because the original human rulers capitulated their dominion to the snake, Satan is now "the god of this world" (2 Cor. 4:4) and "the prince of the power of the air" (Eph. 2:2). The kingdoms of the world are under his sway right now because, in sin, "the whole world lies in the power of the evil one" (1 John 5:19). But this reign of death is illegitimate and parasitic. The cosmos itself is bucking in revolt against this dark power, groaning for the true heirs, "the sons of God" to be revealed in resurrection (Rom. 8:19–21).

Satan's power is twofold. He incites human sin by governing people through "the passions of our flesh, carrying out the desires of the body and the mind" (Eph. 2:3). And he stands as accuser over humanity, keeping us in captivity through fear of death and the coming judgment (Heb. 2:14–15; Rev. 12:10). But with the union of a divine and human nature, Jesus was more than what the old despot could govern. Jesus had neither the darkened mind of his sinful brothers and sisters nor the record of indictment against him. With no guilty conscience to accuse, Jesus could say as he approached the cross, "the ruler of this world is coming. He has no claim on me" (John 14:30).

When offered an empire, Jesus' wisdom cut through to identify immediately the issue at hand—worship. His paraphrased quote of Deuteronomy 6:13–14 cut right to the core of what was happening: "You shall worship the Lord your God and him only shall you serve" (Matt. 4:10).

The context of the Deuteronomy passage was exactly the same as Jesus' vision here on the mountain. God spoke to Israel about the land he was giving them, a kingdom with great glory. The people would be moving into "great and good cities that you did not build, and houses full of all good things that you did not fill, and cisterns that you did not dig, and vineyards and olive trees that you did not plant" (Deut. 6:10–11). The danger for Israel would be to see this as simply the normal state of affairs, to forget that this exaltation was an inheritance, a gift. Once the Israelites believed the kingdom came through their own power, they'd seek more power to maintain it. And that would mean turning to new sources of power—that is, to foreign gods. And behind those gods lurked the unclean angels of Eden's fall.

When Eve, and then Adam, turned from the word of God to believing the word of Satan, they acted as though Satan could be the guarantor of their exaltation. They worshiped him. The nihilism of the fall wasn't simply that the primeval couple ate from the wrong tree. They worshiped the wrong god and thus attacked the entire structure of the divine economy.

The further the Israelites went away from their merciful

rescue from Egypt, the more they showed the same idolatrous instinct. The golden calf incident sums up perfectly the nihilism of human pride. The calf was made of gold, of course, but the Scripture insists that we acknowledge where this gold had come from in the first place. Aaron had taken up an offering of "the rings of gold that are in the ears of your wives, your sons, and your daughters" (Ex. 32:2) Now where did these "rings of gold" come from? The Israelites had plundered this gold jewelry from their Egyptian taskmasters, right before their flight into the night (Ex. 12:35). They did so at the direction of the word of God. And how did it come about? It was because "the LORD had given the people favor in the sight of the Egyptians, so that they let them have what they asked" (Ex. 12:36).

The Israelites used the very gifts God had given them as a weapon against him, the height of entitlement and hubris. This was, of course, precisely what our first ancestors did as well. God created the tree of the knowledge of good and evil. He gave the vegetation to the man and woman to eat. They used the one as a means of insurrection and the other as a hiding place from communion with God. In their pride they'd forgotten they were creatures and subjects and sons and daughters. As the Israelites danced around the golden calf, and in every other instance of worshiping a thing rather than God, they showed they loved their kingdom more than their King. By offering praise to a crafted thing made out of their own stuff, they were "rejoicing in the works of their hands" (Acts 7:41).

Satan was willing to give away his territorial rights to the kingdoms of this world partly because he knew he wouldn't be giving up a kingdom but rather would be gaining another subject. Satan knew from millennia of experience that seeking the kingdom while rejecting the King means losing both.

After all, in Israel's wilderness wandering, God had demonstrated that going after foreign gods meant disinheritance as the people of God (Ex. 23:22–24; Deut. 30:17–20; Josh. 24:14–24). Moreover, Jesus would have been disqualified from kingship. The king, by God's decree, cannot be a self-exalter (Deut. 17:20).

That was the test that Jesus' ancestor had successfully passed in his wilderness sojourn. While Saul saw his kingdom as something to be protected by disregarding God's commands when they seemed to contradict his own purposes and glory (1 Sam. 15:9), David refused to exalt himself by forcing the kingdom, by killing Saul (1 Sam. 24:1–22; 26:8–11). Despite numerous opportunities, David refused to succumb to revenge or bloodlust because he trusted God to keep his promise, to exalt him in due time. Of course, David's kingship ultimately crumbled because even he couldn't maintain humility before God. Instead he used his position as a vehicle for his own sexual release and maintained his unaccountability through fraud and murder to cover it over (2 Sam. 11:1–27).

As Jesus walked into all those stories, he understood what was going on behind the veil in all of them. They were precursors to this very moment. And all those acts of prideful status mongering were really all about one thing—devil worship. Eve was led to see herself as free when she decided to eat of the tree. But she was deceived into believing—ascribing worth to—Satan rather than to the word of God. The Israelites believed themselves to be incorporating the territorial gods of the areas they were conquering. In the case of the golden calf, they just believed they were forging a visible representation of the God they'd known (thus they identified the thing as that which brought them out of Egypt). All they thought they wanted in their idolatries was power and rain and crops and healthy livestock and fertility. They wanted to gain the kingdom and to keep the kingdom. But behind it all they were bowing down to "demons that were no gods" (Deut. 32:17). Behind all the religious syncretism of the kings of Israel, their attempts to exalt their own names or to hold on to their own thrones, there's a common denominator—evil spirits at play behind them (1 Kings 14:21–31; 15:25–16:34).

Satan was asking Jesus to demand the inheritance now (exactly the scenario Jesus recreated in his story of the prodigal son). He wanted Jesus to gain the kingdom by a self-directed word, a word that actually would have been dictated by Satan. Jesus walked into this crisis in order to drive devil worship from the story of man. Satan searched Jesus for pride and self-exaltation and found none there.

Pride is, by definition, idolatrous and insurrectionist because it is rooted in ingratitude. It glorifies the creature over against the Creator and claims the inheritance rights of image-bearers without acknowledging that we have these things because we reflect an image, not because we are ultimate (Rom. 1:22–23). It is the primal sin because no other sin is possible without believing that some good gift of God is mine and mine alone to use for my purposes, for my own kingdom and glory. Satan seeks to replicate his own prideful raging for power in human creatures—that's part of the realm he wants for himself. So the apostle Paul warns Timothy not to set apart a new convert lest he "become puffed up with conceit and fall into the condemnation of the devil" (1 Tim. 3:6).

Most of us know that pride and status-hunger are character flaws. We're irritated when we see it in the self-promoting braggart we know or the preening narcissist in the cubicle next to us. Notice, though, that some of the most arrogant people you know complain about arrogant people. We rarely see the satanism of pride in our own situations.

Part of that is because of how fallen humanity normalizes pride and hubris. Despite all of our fables and legends about the dangers therein—from Icarus to Frankenstein—we grow accustomed to thinking of self-exaltation, at least to some manageable degree, as a "normal" part of leadership and drive. In the business world there's an entire category of books written by psychiatrists to help coworkers and employees navigate around a narcissistic personality, especially in the supervisor or executive. You can't do anything about your boss's self-exaltation, these books uniformly seem to say; just learn to work with him by making sure he thinks every idea you want implemented is his own, and be prepared that if the idea fails it will be said to be someone else's fault. Be ready eventually to be on the outs, because his circle of "stupid" people will eventually expand to include you, these experts say. It's just the way things are.

Often even in Christian ministry the same tendencies are present and covered over in a pretense of humility. Self-promotion and egotism are rewarded because the more a Christian crows about his superior prayer life or his cutting-edge research or his ability to grow churches or movements, the more an audience tends to believe it. Genuine Christian humility, by contrast, often seems mousy or nonassertive by contrast. Sometimes the complaint "he lacks ambition" can be simply translated as "he doesn't worship himself, and he doesn't expect us to either." When so many leaders are proud, it becomes very difficult for the Spirit-convicted psyche to discern, "Am I prideful, or am I a leader?"

Often we're deceived into thinking self-exaltation isn't a weak point for us because we don't see ourselves clamoring for global power or celebrity. But *kingdom* and *glory* are always relative terms. The satanic powers don't care what size kingdom you want or what quantity of glory is enough for you to bow the knee. They just want to see you worship something other than God to get what you want. Philosopher William Irvine argues that "most people seek fame and fortune," just in different ways. "If universal fame eludes them, they seek regional fame, local renown, popularity within their social circle, or distinction among their colleagues," Irvine writes. "Likewise, if they can't amass a fortune in absolute terms, they seek relative affluence: they want to be materially better off than their co-workers, neighbors, relatives, and friends."[3]

For some people, the self-exaltation impulse means fantasizing in front of a mirror about being a world-renowned musician. Others, though, seek the same kind of renown, just limited to the world of air-conditioning repair in West Chester, Ohio. Some people want to be billionaires with villas in the south of France. Others just want their neighbors to envy them because their marriage is intact, their children still in school. The issue isn't the size of the kingdom; it's what you will do to get it. For some it's a future goal, and for others it's a kingdom and glory present only in memory. Think of the middle-aged man who was a high-school athlete and uses his children as a vicarious reincarnation of his own dashed hopes. Think of the woman who seizes her daughter's wedding preparation process in order to recapture the romance she wishes she still had.

Moreover, many of us tend to classify "pride" and "status seeking" as something that befalls obviously arrogant people. You can probably think right now of someone in your life who is "that guy," the haughty know-it-all who begins every other sentence with the word "actually . . ." You know what it is to hear that woman in the department store tell her friends, "I'll see you all in a little while; you know I have to shop in the 'petite' section." These obvious manifestations, though, aren't the only aspects of human pride. This is, after all, "common to man" (1 Cor. 10:13). Regardless of your level of self-confidence, you are grappling with this temptation right now, unless you've already succumbed to it. Envy is a form of pride. You don't have to succeed at one thing to see the kingdoms and glory you think you ought to have—and to pine for it inside. Some of the least prideful people you know—those paralyzed by worry, anxiety, or indecisiveness—are the most prideful, and for exactly the reasons you think they're not.

I've never had a devil tattoo, but I do have ongoing marks of my struggle with satanism. They are yellow highlights in an old King James Bible my grandmother gave me when I turned twelve. Unlike the upside-down cross, they weren't marks of desecration but marks of devotion. I was doing just what a Southern Baptist teenager was supposed to do—having a daily "quiet time" of prayer and Bible reading, making notes to myself. But I hate to look at some of those highlighted verses.

In almost every case I can tell what was going on in my life that prompted me to be drawn to the particular highlighted verse. The highlight over "I can do all things through Christ which strengtheneth me" (Phil. 4:13 KJV) was because I was worried sick that I'd fail geometry class (I passed—barely). When I see the highlight over the verse "Whatsoever ye shall ask in my name, that will I do" (John 14:13 KJV) was because I was praying (and repeating "in Jesus' name" after every clause, to hold God to his promise here) for God to let this girl in my homeroom become interested enough in me to become my girlfriend (God didn't; and I'm glad). The highlight over 1 Samuel 16:7 ("Look not on his countenance, or on the height of his stature . . . for the LORD seeth not as man seeth; for man looketh on the outward appearance, but the LORD looketh on the heart," KJV) was because I'm a little cricket of a man, and I was hoping to grow tall enough at least to be considered for the basketball team (that didn't happen).

Now there is nothing wrong with praying through the Bible for what concerns you, of course. But those highlights remind me just how dominated my life was at the time by worry and anxiety. I was not at all what anyone would consider proud or arrogant (I don't think, although that may just be my pride keeping me from seeing it!), but the pride and exaltation in my little Bible-reading frame morphed into other smaller (and thus more dangerous) forms of hubris and lust for power. I wanted my little kingdoms secure and within my grasp, and when they didn't seem to be, I was agitated, if not outraged.

Sometimes the kingdom Satan is killing you with isn't what you're basking in but what you're worrying about. Jesus, though, was free from devil worship because he was free from worry. He understood both his Father's care and that exaltation must come at "the proper time" (1 Pet. 5:6), a time not of his own choosing. Jesus has told us that even by looking at the natural world—the ecosystems of birds and plants and fields—we can see an icon of God's inheritance—"even Solomon in all his glory was not arrayed like one of these" (Matt. 6:29). Since you don't need to grasp for power or glory—God is freely preparing you for it—instead you're free to "seek first the kingdom of God and his righteousness, and all these things will be added to you" (Matt. 6:33).

The pull to self-exaltation can also show up in the ease

with which you take offense. Essayist David Brooks, picking up on contemporary psychological models for clinical narcissism, notes that for the narcissist the self-image is "the holy center of all that is sacred and right." This affects then how the narcissist receives criticism and personal offense. "If someone treats him slightingly, he perceives that as a deliberate and heinous attack," Brooks writes. "If someone threatens his reputation, he regards this as an act of blasphemy."[4] Blasphemy is precisely the right word. The reason the offense becomes so all-consuming is that it is an attack on one's god and on one's kingdom—the self-image. As we worship God instead of ourselves, we will find that the love of Christ "is not easily angered" but instead "keeps no record of wrongs" (1 Cor. 13:5 NIV).

Jesus knew he would receive the kingdoms of this world and all their glory. And he knew how he would receive them. It wasn't by a secret knowledge or a cunning strategy, and it certainly wasn't by finding a substitute god. Jesus knew the promise that God had made to David about David's son: "Ask of me, and I will make the nations your heritage, and the ends of the earth your possession" (Ps. 2:8). The psalmist sang God's promise to the Davidic king: "He shall cry to me, 'You are my Father, my God, and the Rock of my salvation.' And I will make him the firstborn, the highest of the kings of the earth" (Ps. 89:26–27). Jesus knew that the kingdom we are born craving doesn't come through our designs; it comes through asking: "Your kingdom come, your will be done, on earth as it is in heaven" (Matt. 6:10).

That's because the kingdom that's coming cannot be occupied by the proud. The kingdom is, by definition, other directed. God the Father exalts the name of the Son, building for him a kingdom (2 Sam. 7:13–14) and putting all his enemies under his feet. Jesus the Son fights for the kingdom in order that he may hand it over to his Father, "that God may be all in all" (1 Cor. 15:28). The Spirit calls out subjects of the kingdom and fuels the prayers for the kingdom, so that the Christ of God might be magnified (John 14). In every case, the kingdom of God is other directed, not self-consumed.

In this coming kingdom, nothing satanic will enter (Rev. 21:27). "The haughty looks of man shall be brought low, and the lofty pride of men shall be humbled," Isaiah announced, "and the Lord alone will be exalted in that day" (Isa. 2:11). God actively opposes the proud (James 4:6). Jesus knew that if he bowed the knee to Satan, he would be disqualified from the inheritance, since no idol worshiper will enter the kingdom of God (1 Cor. 6:9–10). Instead it is the "meek" who will inherit the universe (Ps. 37:11; Matt. 5:5).

But "meek" doesn't mean mousy. Jesus in his third temptation actually refused to be humbled. The ancient prophecy was true: "The enemy shall not outwit him; the wicked shall not humble him" (Ps. 89:22). Jesus knew that God would exalt him precisely because he humbled himself to his Father's good purposes (Isa. 52:13; Phil. 2:8–9). Jesus would bow the knee to his Father, but to no one else.

Because God is at war with Satan and the occupying powers of this universe, we don't have any option but to crucify our kingdom-building. If you are outside of Christ, God will patiently endure with you, offering you another way. But if you persist, your kingdom—whatever it is—will collapse around you in death. The writing is on the wall (Dan. 5:1–30).

If you are in Christ, God will not allow you to enter his reign with a kingdom-grasping pride. You will be stripped of every haughty look, every personal empire, in order that you might enter as a little child, looking for a Father's inheritance. This will come either through personal repentance, learning to humble yourself, or by God's humbling you through his working it out in your life to knock down your empire so that you can be found in his.

The Spirit then applies the exact same mind of Christ from the desert to us now. Since that's the case, the Bible commands us, "Do nothing from rivalry or conceit, but in humility count others more significant than yourselves" (Phil. 2:3). If future rule and future glory is before us, then why would we settle for being the most acclaimed future corpse in our little corner of the world?

This counter satanic humility can be seen, first, in Christians learning to give up the sense of desperation we feel when we lose "control" of our lives, our expectations, our families, our churches, our country. I don't know what your personal trap is for kingdom building. For me, the satanic temptation was there in the having of children. When my wife and I first married, I was absolutely terrified of her getting pregnant "too early." I had all kinds of plans for my schooling and for my ministry, and I didn't think we could "afford" children for a while. The day finally arrived when I was "ready" to be a father. Maria and I made the "decision" and celebrated around the table. It was almost like an engagement. But nothing happened. Thank God.

That's easy for me to say two adoptions and two births—four children later. But if we had conceived right away, I would have been a miserably bad father. I would have seen those children as simply an extension of myself and of my plans for the future. I know that because of the way I reacted to years of infertility and miscarriage. Although I never would have put it this way, I actually felt as though God was taking something away from me. He was taking away from me the "normal" life I'd mapped out for myself. In fact, he was taking away from me my god, the god of a self-directed future. And behind all that was a reptilian spirit. I don't know what you're being offered right now, but you'll either surrender it or you'll collapse right along with it. Whatever you're concerned about will lead you to what you'll worship. And on what you worship hinges your destiny.

Self-denying humility ought to show up in the way we worship together. Thankfully, we don't hear as much these days about worship wars in Christian churches as we did just a few years ago, but they are still there. For years I thought this phenomenon was the bane of the "make it up as you go along" whirl of low-church evangelical Protestantism, and mostly it is. But even with a set traditional liturgy, Roman Catholics and other groups often experience the same kinds of tensions.

Maybe you're like me, reared to have the worship music tastes of a seventy-five-year-old woman. That's because, I think, a seventy-five-year-old woman was picking out the hymns and gospel songs in the church where I grew up. I tear up when I sing "Just As I Am" or "To God Be the Glory." And I'm left cold by what some people call the "majestic old hymns." They sound like what watercress-sandwich-eating Episcopalians from Connecticut would listen to (not that there's anything wrong with that). And so many of the contemporary songs sound as if they were written by commercial jingle writers, trying desperately to find words to rhyme with "Jesus" ("Sees us?" "Never leave us?" "Diseases?"). I'm not saying aesthetics don't matter in worship. Worship is, after all, commanded to be offered with "reverence and awe" (Heb. 12:28). I am saying our varying critiques of musical forms are often just simple narcissism disguised as concern about theological and liturgical downgrade.

We need more worship wars, not fewer. What if the war looked like this in your congregation—the young singles petitioning the church to play more of the old classics for the sake of the elderly people, and the elderly people calling on the leadership to contemporize for the sake of the young new believers? This would signal a counting of others as more important than ourselves (Phil. 2:3), which comes from the Spirit of the humiliated, exalted King, Christ (Phil. 2:5–11). When I insist that the rest of the congregation serve as backup singers in my own little nostalgic hit parade of back-home Mississippi hymns, I am worshiping in the spirit all right, but not the Holy Spirit. I am worshiping myself, in the spirit of self-exaltation. The church negates the power of the third temptation when we remind ourselves that we all have this devilish tendency and cast it aside whether in worship planning or missions or budget decisions.

The narcissistic soul has, we're told by those who observe such things, a basic lack of empathy, an inability to feel what another is feeling or to even see the other except in terms of an extension of oneself. At the end of its malignancy, the self-exalting soul screams out the blasphemous words of Satan: "I am, and there is no one besides me" (Isa. 47:10; Zeph. 2:15). But Narcissus is drowned in the baptismal waters. When we give up our own craving for power and glory, we find new power and new glory in Christ. We worship God and let our kingdoms fall. In order for the Christocracy to come, the "ego-ocracies" must be crucified.

A QUESTION OF MISSION

Why would Satan be willing to negotiate away his empire for thirty seconds of adoration? The other two temptations, arguably, cost the Devil nothing. This one is conditioned on his giving away the very thing he craves most—power and glory. And why could Jesus not simply acknowledge Satan's rightful rule over the people who bear his sonship, a momentary giving of honor in order to trick him away from his illegitimate birthright? Jesus, after all, elsewhere acknowledges Satan as "the ruler of this world" (John 12:31). The very reason Jesus appeared was "to destroy the works of the devil" (1 John 3:8). Jesus could have destroyed them with a moment's bended knee, right? The answer is found not only in Jesus' quotation about the exclusive worship of God but also in his prefatory statement: "Be gone, Satan."

The word *Satan* means "adversary." The natural question is, "adversary to what?" Of course, Satan is the adversary of all of God's purposes. He is the adversary of all God's people. But where do God's purposes for his people and for his universe find their climax? They find it in the gospel of a bloody cross and an emptied tomb. Jesus used the proper name "Satan" in the same way he would later, when it seemed that Satan wasn't around at all. Jesus' follower Peter said, when he heard Jesus talking about his coming arrest and execution, that he would never let that happen. That sounds awfully commendable to me, I have to admit. If I were musing aloud about the possibility of my being murdered, I'd kind of like my friends to say something along the lines of "Not while we're here. We're watching out for you." When Peter does this, though, Jesus spits out the words, "Get behind me, Satan!" (Matt. 16:21–23). Why?

It was because Jesus was speaking to another voice behind Peter's voice. Peter wanted to protect Jesus' kingdom by navigating around the cross. In that evasion of crucifixion, Jesus heard something he'd heard before, something satanic to the core. What was at stake in the third temptation was the gospel.

Think about the implications of this offer. If Jesus had accepted it, Satan would have surrendered his reign of terror. Jesus could have directed the kingdoms of the world however he wanted. No more babies would be miscarried. No more women would die in childbirth. Ended immediately would be all human slavery, all genocide, all disease, all poverty, all torture, and all ecological catastrophes. The rows and rows of crosses across the highway of the Roman Empire would suddenly be gone. There would never be a Nero or a Napoleon or a Hitler or a Stalin, or at least you would never hear the infamy of those names. There would be no world of divorce courts and abortion clinics and electric chairs and pornographic images. Whatever is troubling you right now would be gone, centuries before you were ever conceived. This sounds like paradise.

Satan was willing to give all of this up because he doesn't fear Christianity. He certainly doesn't fear "Christian values." Satan fears Christ. Remember that Satan holds power only through accusation and condemnation. As long as there is no atoning sacrifice for sin, Satan is quite willing to allow conformity to the external law, even to the law of Christ ruling visibly over the nations from Jerusalem. The accuser simply wants his opportunity to indict his human would-be supplanting powers before the judgment seat, with no shed blood to redeem them back.

This is what Jesus' followers couldn't understand as he moved down the Roman roads toward the place of the skull. It was there, and only there, as Jesus carried on himself the sins of the world, that he could say, "Now is the judgment of this world; now will the ruler of this world be cast out" (John 12:31). It is only in his triumphant resurrection from the demonic grip of death that Jesus could have "angels, authorities, and powers" subjected to his rule (1 Pet. 3:21–22). A crossless Christianity isn't just a deficient Christianity; it's the same old satanism of human striving.

The apostolic mandate then was to "know nothing among you except Jesus Christ and him crucified" (1 Cor. 2:2). Of course, the apostles spoke of many other things besides the basic gospel message—church leadership, family order, sexuality, the Christian's life in society and the marketplace, and so on. But all of that was in the context of the overarching story of the universe: God's deliverance of the world from Satan's accusation through the atoning blood and ongoing life of Jesus Christ. This is why the apostles rejected personal power bases—what the contemporary evangelical subculture would call "branding"—for themselves. "Was Paul crucified for you?" Paul asked in 1 Corinthians 1:13 with a desperate kind of sarcasm to the celebrity-seeking church at Corinth.

In every generation the church faces cross-evading liberation theologies of both the Left and the Right. The liberation theology of the Left wants a Barabbas to fight off the oppressors, as though the ultimate problem is the reign of Rome and not the reign of death. The liberation theology of the Right wants a golden calf to represent religion and "traditional values" in the public square and to remind us of all the economic security we could have in Egypt. Both want a Caesar or a Pharaoh, not a Messiah.

We will always be tempted to bypass the problem behind the problems—captivity to sin, bondage to the accusations of the demonic powers, the sentence of death. Where there is no gospel, something else will fill the void—therapy, consumerism, racial resentment, utopian politics, crazy conspiracy theories of the Left, crazy conspiracy theories of the Right; anything will do. Where there is something other than Christ preached, there is no freedom. There may be shouts of affirmation or silently nodding heads. There may be left-wing politics or right-wing politics. There may be culturally liberal psychotherapy or culturally conservative psychotherapy. There may be almost anything people think they want, but there's nothing but judgment in the air.

The Devil doesn't mind "family values" as long as what you ultimately value is the family. Satan doesn't mind "social justice" as long as you see justice as most importantly social. Satan does not tremble at a "Christian worldview" as long as your ultimate goal is to view the world. Satan doesn't even mind born-again Christianity as long as the new birth is preached apart from the blood of the cross and the life of the resurrection.

Pastor, Satan doesn't mind if you preach on the decrees of God with fervor and passion, reconciling all the tensions between sovereignty and freedom, as long as you don't preach the gospel. Homeschooling mom, Satan doesn't mind if your children can recite the catechism and translate the "Battle Hymn of the Republic" from English to Latin, as long as they don't hear the gospel. Churches, Satan doesn't care if your people vote for pro-life candidates, stay married, have sex with whom they're supposed to, and tear up at all the praise choruses, as long as they don't see the only power that cancels condemnation—the gospel of Christ crucified. Satan so fears that gospel, he was willing to surrender his entire empire just to stave it off. He still is.

To say that a truly Christian witness must be crucified is not to say that our witness must fit neatly into the categories some would deem as "spiritual." As regular as rain in the history of the church, another cycle of utopian-politicized Christians—of either the Right or the Left—emerges. And with the same regularity the next generation is disillusioned with the hubris of it all and with the inevitably disappointing results. They then call for a retreat from social and political engagement. We should simply preach the gospel, they say. Trying desperately to prove they are not their parents, these "gospel-only" Christians dismiss concerns for public justice or social conscience as either culture wars or social gospel. In some cases, they are right about the particulars of their critiques, but the separatist isolationism of these "gospel-only" movements doesn't escape the third temptation. It gives in to it vigorously, just from another direction.

The "apolitical" churches in history are typically the most political of all, despite themselves. The white leaders demanding a depoliticized "spirituality of the church" in the era of American slavery weren't eschewing worldly power. They were embracing it. The "simple gospel preaching" churches of the Jim Crow South who didn't want to say something as political as a stance on lynching laws or the Ku Klux Klan were propping up the white supremacist power structure that benefited them. They weren't transcending the carnal power around them; they just refused to challenge it, opting to preach on "personal" morality issues like drinking and dancing and card playing while the corpses of their black neighbors swung from ropes in the trees outside.

The road to Damascus is not a different path from the road to Jericho. The proclamation of love of neighbor is not incidental to gospel proclamation, as though it were some kind of secondary implication of the gospel. Jesus, after all, told the story of the Samaritan who cared for his mugged and beaten neighbor in the context of a religious leader who was "desiring to justify himself" (Luke 10:29). That man evaded his own sin by doing precisely what the Devil did with the commands of God, interpreting them around his own conscience: "Who is my neighbor?" Should we rebuke Jesus for neglecting the gospel for social ministry? God forbid. Jesus was pointing out the very roots of human sin, contrasting it with the righteousness of God. There is no gospel apart from that.

In the attempt to protect the gospel from being too big, some Christians undercut the gospel and bypass the cross just as surely, if not more so, as their hyperpolitical Christian activist cousins. The gospel cannot be understood without an awareness of sin. Gospel preaching means defining what the kingdom of God is and what it is not and defining as rebellion what God calls rebellion. Sin includes what we sometimes dismiss as social or political concerns—such as unjust workers' wages (Lev. 19:13; Deut. 24:15; James 5:4–5), usury (Lev. 25:35–37; Neh. 5:6–10), abuse of the land (Jer. 2:7; Hos. 4:1–3), and mistreatment of the poor, the elderly, the sojourners, the widows, and the orphans (Ex. 22:22; Deut. 10:18; Ezek. 16:49; Zech. 7:10; James 1:27).

It is true that Scripture does not, in many instances, give us a detailed blueprint of how to approach such issues at a societal or governmental level. We allow then for Christians to form their consciences in conversation about the most prudent course. But that doesn't mean we can simply dismiss such concerns as tangential to our primary concern. Christians have differing opinions about when and whether divorce and remarriage is allowed or about whether contraception or masturbation is ever ethically acceptable. Do we then simply say, "We're not going to address marriage or sexuality—we're going to stay focused on the gospel"?

An adulterer who refuses to repent of his adultery is defying the gospel. A child-trafficker who refuses to repent of her child trafficking is defying the gospel. One who steals another's property—whether through coercion or by poisoning the water on it—and who refuses to repent of his mistreatment of his neighbor is defying the gospel. The gospel doesn't just proclaim, "Your sins are forgiven"; the gospel also exposes the answer to the question, who is my neighbor? The gospel marginalizes the power of every society, every state, and every person by announcing the criteria for judgment.

If our mission is centered on the cross, we will still address social and political concerns, but we will do so without concern for our own power or influence. This will mean a certain prophetic distance from powers that be. Have you ever noticed that in our present context, the social and political categories are so monolithic and predictable, even when the internal coherences keep changing? Progressives were originally "pro-life," and conservatives were "antiwar," but as time goes on and different people come to power, those things change. Why does Christian witness so often morph right along with the political evolutions? Why are evangelicals with a concern for poverty expected to minimize the abortion issue (even if they insist they're still pro-life)? Why are evangelicals with a concern for the life of the unborn expected to be predictably in line with whatever is considered to be "conservative" at the moment on any issue from the minimum wage to the torture of enemy combatants? Why are people who care about conserving the earth's ecology supposed to be silent about preserving a healthy moral ecology of the natural family and intact marriage?

I suspect this is because doing anything else would marginalize your access to the elite level, to the people who grant you the influence you need to continue to have a place at the table. Once alliances are made, the allies adopt an approach of "the enemy of the enemy is my friend." At the root is a quest, it seems, for kingdom and glory, accessible by joining the right team and asserting your power within the rules of that team's internal narrative. It is hard to see that this has strengthened the credibility of Christian witness in virtually any arena.

Whatever prophetic voice we offer, though, must be for the purpose of the gospel of the kingdom, not for the purpose of gaining—or keeping—influence with whatever powers—social, political, intellectual, cultural—that we wish to impress. It is not enough, therefore, to condemn racism. We must love the racial supremacist enough to call him to repentance in order to offer him forgiveness through the blood of Christ. It is not enough to work to end abortion. We must demonstrate to women who've had abortions that there is no condemnation for them—none—if they are hidden in Christ. It's not enough to care for orphans and widows and the elderly and the poor. We must do so while offering the whole world the opportunity to find a home in a kingdom made up of those who are lame and blind and lost.

The same dynamic is in effect when it comes to the church's concern for cultural influence. Some Christians have rightly determined that the world is shaped less by politics than by culture. Some have sought to move Christian witness from the failed experiment of a voting bloc to an incarnational presence in the visual arts, music, dance, film, and so on. These Christians seek to transcend the self-referential and consumerist era of often kitschy "Christian art." Insofar as this empowers the people of Christ to love God and neighbor and to love what God loves, including beauty, it should be commended. But the third temptation will always be just around the bend. There will be the lure to see artistic acclaim at the most elite levels itself as a way of distinguishing ourselves from the rabble in our churches. Some have even suggested that Christians move en masse to the cultural epicenters, New York and Los Angeles, in order to change the culture.

Yes, we need Christians in New York and Los Angeles, and we should cultivate those gifted to work in the arts in those places. But we don't necessarily need the applause of Madison Avenue and Hollywood, and we probably aren't going to get it. We also should avoid rejecting that which the regnant culture dismisses, such as rural people and country folkways.

Besides, the most truly transformative art is rarely received by the ambient culture in the lifetime of the artist. And transformative art does not always come from the elite and powerful culture mavens. Think, for instance, of the slave spirituals and Appalachian bluegrass and Russian dissident literature. We should cultivate culture influencers in the same way the apostles cultivated the Christians among the Praetorian Guard and the aristocracy. But at the same time we must remember that most of the apostles themselves were not "culture-shapers" but commercial fishermen and low-level government contractors. The Christian movement that shaped the cultures of empires and kingdoms and nations was not made up initially of many who were noble or powerful or even respectable (1 Cor. 1:26).

There are always, especially in my wing of conservative

Christianity, those who gain an audience with an "Ain't it awful" kind of pessimistic jeremiad about the future of Christian witness. Usually when it's stripped down to the raw nub of the argument, this is about a loss of influence for the church, which should be read as a loss of power and glory. Some say the day is arriving when Christian America won't be able to count on billionaire donors to fund all our ministries and monuments. They say Christian leaders will be too "radioactive" to be invited to the White House. Politicians won't seek our opinions or ask for our church directories for direct-mail campaigns. If that is what Christian America is about, then let it collapse. Or better yet, let it be crucified. Let's lose that kind of influence so we can seek first the kingdom of God and the countercultural power and glory that goes with it.

But the future of Christ's church is hopeful, indeed thrillingly so. Where the gospel is preached, where the whole story of Scripture is summed up in Christ, where reconciliation is modeled, there Jesus will build his church. And people will there find authenticity and wholeness and liberation. But God will, as he always does, raise up the humble and knock down the prideful. Perhaps that's why the most vital Christianity is increasingly found in the so-called Third World, with believers too pinned in by persecution to fall for power worship, whether of the covetous revolutionary or jealous consumerist kinds.

The first step of any kind of Christian engagement with the outside world then is to focus on the primary arena of Christ's reign—his church. We threaten the rulers and authorities in the heavenly places by our life together, by being the kind of alternative community that demonstrates that the blood of Christ has triumphed, making those who were at odds into one new reality in Christ (Eph. 3:9–12).

The Bible says that when Jesus left from the temptations in the desert, he went back to Galilee (Matt. 4:12–16; Luke 4:14), to the backward little community that would have been the complete antithesis of the kingdoms and the glory he'd just seen in the satanic vision. And from there he announced a new kingdom's dawn (Matt. 4:15–17; Luke 4:16–22).

What would it mean if the leadership structures of our churches weren't as predictable as the leadership structures of every other organization in our communities? What would the outside world say if they saw, in the pictures of our Christian publications, people who would be rejected by the advertising industry for being too fat or too pimply or too awkward? What would our neighbors think, to see that our chairman of deacons has Down syndrome or that a minimum-wage janitor is mentoring the millionaire executive of the hotel chain where he cleans toilets? It would look awfully strange. But it would look no stranger than a starving, homeless wilderness wanderer turning down the opportunity to rule the world.

CONCLUSION

Jesus said to the Devil, "Be gone," and he was gone. Matthew tells us simply, "Then the devil left him" (Matt. 4:10–11). But he didn't leave for good. The old spirit lurked around repeatedly in the Gospel accounts, and in the fullness of time he entered one of Jesus' followers, kicking off the path to crucifixion. That crucifixion all hinged on those seconds in the desert when the Galilean refused to bow down to a reptile. Jesus turned down glory and power because he was going to a cross. And so are you.

You probably don't think of yourself as having much power, certainly not the kind of power you sometimes wish you had. But if you're in Christ, you are a galactic emperor in training. You are being shaped and matured in order to reign with Christ from his throne (Rev. 2:26–27). Your present sojourn through this time of temptation and trial is a kind of boot camp. If you are faithful in small things, you'll be given authority over great things (Matt. 25:23).

But the self-exalting ego cannot enter the reign of God, no matter how powerful it seems right now, no matter how normal it seems in the present. Narcissism is satanism. Self-exaltation is devil worship. Satan's power will only stand for a flash of time, and that time is growing shorter (Rev. 12:12). The power of the cross doesn't simply replace our power seeking with a new niche for the power. Our lust for personal kingdom building isn't simply counterproductive—it's demonic at the root. You don't have to claw and connive for power and glory. In Christ, God is preparing you for more power and glory than you can comprehend right now. You've freed them from your cunning and your anxiety. "Fear not," Jesus tells us, "for it is your Father's good pleasure to give you the kingdom" (Luke 12:32).

The satanic powers are watching you. They're peering into your life to see what catches your attention, what puffs up your ego. They're evaluating what kind of Babylon you want to build for yourself, and they'll make sure you get it. Satan is as ambitious for your goals as you are, maybe more so. He'll give you the power you want, the glory you crave, as long as you will fall down and obtain it his way. The powers don't care if we are respected or influential or moral or conservative, as long as we'd rather be magnified than crucified. Satan doesn't mind if our values are right side up, so long as our crosses are upside-down.

6

WHERE THE WILD THINGS AREN'T

Why You Can Resist Temptation
(Especially If You Can't See How)

If you ever pass by on the sidewalk outside my house and you hear four young boys (and one grown man) howling like animals inside, I'll go ahead and tell you now, don't be unnerved. It just means it's family devotion time at our place. In our home, family worship isn't very structured, and it sure isn't dignified. My sons and I wrestle, we tell stories, we hear from the Scriptures, we pray for one another, and then, on some special nights, after our Bible reading we pull down from the shelf a book that's been a favorite of my sons since they were babies, and it gets kind of wild.

As soon as I start reading *Where the Wild Things Are* by Maurice Sendak, it gets quiet.[1] My sons have heard this tale since they were babies, about a boy around their age named Max who is sent to his room for telling his mother he'll eat her up. They start shifting around in their seats as they hear about his room becoming a forest, about his encountering scary, teeth-baring "wild things." They bounce up and bay along with the creatures as they hear once again about Max's adventures there in that faraway land, and usually before I can even get to the text on the page, one of them will jump up and scream, "Let the wild rumpus start!"

And it does.

My boys aren't unusual. When I was their age, I loved this story as much as they do. And as I talk to people about my age, I find that this book struck—and strikes—a particular resonance with at least two generations of American children, no matter what their racial, social, economic, or religious backgrounds. Why?

If, as both ancient and contemporary wisdom tell us, stories exist to help us categorize our fears and aspirations, then "wild" children's stories remind us of what we see everywhere in human art—from cave paintings to country music to the Cannes Film Festival: we're afraid of the wildness "out there" in the scary universe around us. Whether we fear saber-toothed tigers or Wall Street collapse or malaria or our parents' impending divorce, there are frightening, threatening forces out there that seem outside of our control.

And worse than that, we seem to fear, perhaps most of all, the uncontrollable "wildness" inside of us—those passions and desires and rages and longings and sorrows within our psyches that seem to be even scarier because they're so hidden, so close, and so much at the core of who we are. The wildness within us doesn't seem to end, either. It just morphs throughout the life cycle from toddler-age tantrums to teenage hormones to midlife crises and beyond.

Such stories—and they are legion, in every culture—show us what we seem to know intuitively—that the wildness, both out there and in here, needs to be governed. The wildness needs to be reined in, and reigned in. We need a king, and we need to be part of a kingdom. After all, Max only gains power over his "wild things" when he gains self-control, control that comes with his being named "king of all the wild things."

If only it were that easy.

The children's "wild things stories" were fresh in my mind one morning a couple of years ago when a friend and I were talking. The first thing I noticed was that he wouldn't look at me. He stared at his hands as he flexed them open and shut, telling me he was going to hell. When I asked why, my friend (let's call him Felix) said it was because he was on the edge of apostasy, all the time. "Well, I am too," I replied. "No, you don't understand," he said. "It's really bad."

Felix told me that he battled against the pull to do stuff, awful stuff. When I pressed Felix about the gospel, he seemed to evidence credible faith and repentance. But he wanted me to know just how dark his demons were inside. "If you could prove to me that Jesus' bones were in the ground in the Middle East," he said, "I'd leave here right now and get as drunk as I could get, take every drug I could find, and sleep with every woman who would let me." I think he was a little surprised when I chimed back, "Me too."

I told Felix that if the bones of Jesus were in the ground, it seems to me his response is exactly what we ought to do: "Let us eat and drink, for tomorrow we die" (1 Cor. 15:32). The question rather than that is this: "Do you, in fact, believe the bones of Jesus are in the ground?" Felix's eyes welled up with tears that he manfully blinked away. "No, I believe he's alive," he said. "And that's why I fight this stuff all the time." Let me give you a formal theological term for what Felix is experiencing: the normal Christian life.

In our conversation, it was hardly that he was the struggler and I was the sage. As a matter of fact, his anguish was my anguish too. I was able to see it clearly in his case, but not so clearly in mine. We are both like the little boy in the children's story—staring down our wildnesses, hoping to become king over it.

As I've been writing this book, I've thought a lot about the memorable images from that children's book. Jesus, after all, faced temptation in the wild places, the wilderness. As a matter of fact, the Gospel of Mark tells us, somewhat inexplicably, that "he was with the wild animals" there (Mark 1:13). And there Jesus experienced what our sagas and legends and children's tales can only imagine. He became king of all the wild things by silencing the wildness with words. The Word came into the world, and the wildness has not overcome it.

I know, though, that as you read this book, you might be asking the question, "But what can I do?" Perhaps you're looking at whatever is bedeviling you right now, and what you'd like is a series of steps that will quickly and decisively put the temptation behind you. There are some world religions and some philosophies, old and new, that might seek to outline such steps. The Christian gospel, however, will point you only to Christ.

This doesn't mean, however, that there's not a way to follow, a means to resist temptation. In a letter to the church at Corinth, less than a generation after the ascension of Jesus to the heavenly places, the apostle Paul turned to the question of fighting back the wildness. Paul told them what was at stake for them—a wrestling with demons (1 Cor. 10:20) that comes through the disciplining action of a Father God (1 Cor. 11:32). Fitting these Christians into the larger story of temptation and triumph, the apostle called them to resist, and to resist through the gospel. Wildness isn't unusual, he wrote. Their temptations, no matter how freakish they may seem, are "common to man" (1 Cor. 10:13). Moreover, none of them are too powerful to be resisted.

But how do we do this? We resist temptation the way Jesus did, through the word of the kingdom. As we follow Jesus, we see the gospel reclaim our identity, reorder our desires, and reframe our future. We need to recognize that we are living in a war zone, a cosmos being ripped from the dominion of its demonic overlords. We are right now part of a counterinsurgency through the mission of Christ. It's only in this way that we see the power of temptation over us broken, as the demonic powers flee from the presence of the only Man they fear.

RECLAIMING YOUR IDENTITY

My friend Felix's problem was the same one that most people face at some point or another. His expectations of Christianity were both too high and too low. This is precisely where the satanic powers want to pin you, to hubris or to despair. As a matter of fact, the best situation the demons can have you in is actually a combination of the two, in which you ricochet back and forth between them. The gospel, though, reorients our view of ourselves, of God, and of the world by telling us who we are in Christ.

When the apostle Paul warned the Corinthian believers about temptation, he prefaced his comments with these words: "For I want you to know, brothers, that our fathers were all under the cloud, and all passed through the sea, and all were baptized into Moses in the cloud and in the sea" (1 Cor. 10:1–2). This points, first of all, to humility.

From what we can tell from the rest of Paul's letter to the Corinthians, the people to whom he was writing persisted in eclipsing the gospel with a sense of personal hubris. Paul silenced such boasting by reciting the truth of the gospel—no one comes to God except by receiving the undeserved mercy found in the crucifixion and resurrection of Jesus Christ. If this is so, Paul wrote, then why did they brag and boast as though they hadn't been given this as a gift (1 Cor. 1:26–31; 4:7)?

This hubris is especially dangerous when it comes to temptation. Our forefathers and foremothers were all "baptized." What did Paul mean by this? They had all, he said, gone through the cloud and through the sea, referencing the Israelites' escape from Egyptian tyranny through the parted waters. They had seen the dynamism of God's exodus delivery. And yet most of them ended up as rotting corpses in the wilderness. If they fell, Paul wrote, then certainly so can you.

"Therefore," Paul wrote, "let anyone who thinks that he stands take heed lest he fall" (1 Cor. 10:12). That is, in fact, what baptism is all about, an "appeal to God for a good conscience" (1 Pet. 3:21). Your baptism is a sign that you've been buried with Christ (Col. 2:12). Like your ancestors pinned up against the sea, the only thing that has delivered you is the power of God. That repentance then ought to be ongoing, continually reminding you that you are capable of any sin. You are invulnerable to nothing. Pretending so only drives you further to destruction.

This is one reason why the New Testament is filled with the gospel. Too often contemporary Christians assume the gospel is merely a tool used by Christians to convince unbelievers to repent of sin and to trust in Christ. But the churches at Rome, Corinth, Galatia, Ephesus, Philippi, Thessalonica, and so on were clearly made up of believers (the Bible says so), and yet the apostles were continually rehearsing the gospel for them. Was this simply to help them rehearse their next evangelistic encounter? No, it was because a believer is united to Christ through the faith that comes through the gospel, and that faith (and repentance) is a persistent reality in the Christian life. The gospel shows me, at the first revelation of Christ to me, that I'm a sinner. It continues to show me this throughout my life as a believer.

Felix's assurance was troubled because he, like so many Christians, was disturbed by his temptation and his need for repentance. But that's what the gospel does. "If we say we have no sin, we deceive ourselves, and the truth is not in us," the apostle John wrote. "If we confess our sins, he is faithful and just to forgive us our sins and to cleanse us from all unrighteousness" (1 John 1:8–9). Sometimes when the convicting power of the gospel hits, we see this blessing as a sign that God is far from us when, in fact, the conviction in the midst of temptation means the exact opposite. When we are tempted to think of ourselves as beyond temptation, the gospel asks us again, "Who do you think you are?"

The gospel does bring about humility, but the gospel is, of course, by definition good news. Consider again Paul's words to the Corinthians: "For I want you to know, brothers, that our fathers were all under the cloud, and all passed through the sea, and all were baptized into Moses in the cloud and in the sea" (1 Cor. 10:1–2). If this doesn't cause us to stand with jaws agape in awe, it is only because we've grown so accustomed to the gospel or because we don't have any idea what it is.

The words "brothers" and "our fathers" here are striking. Paul, after all, was writing to Gentiles, some of whom, if not most of whom, weren't genetically or culturally related to the Israelites of the exodus at all. They were outsiders, foreigners to the promises of the Bible, who nonetheless had come, somehow, to believe in Jesus. Paul reminded them, though, that in Christ they were the offspring of Abraham. They were "brothers" now, and they shared a story line with Jesus, a story line that reshaped how they were to see themselves.

The Corinthians, even though they were uncircumcised and were probably judged by Jewish believers around them as "pagan," weren't in the church accidentally. They weren't spectators of the biblical story. As a matter of fact, the events of the Bible happened, in part, precisely because God knew they'd be there. "Now these things took place as examples for us," Paul wrote. "Now these things happened to them as an example, but they were written down for our instruction, on whom the end of the ages has come" (1 Cor. 10:6, 11).

Think about that for a minute. It's not just that the Bible is relevant to your ongoing struggle against whatever is tempting you. God in his manifold wisdom knew that you would be here. He knew whatever it is that would bedevil you. This knowledge was part of his mysterious reason for allowing the story of redemption to happen as it did and for his writing it down and preserving it through the millennia. That means there is nothing in your life, not even your most animalistic hidden temptation, that isn't taken into account in the Word of the gospel that addresses you. And he addresses you anyway, saying of you, if you're in Christ, in the gospel, exactly what he says of our Lord Jesus: "This is my beloved child, in whom I am well pleased."

Moreover, Paul showed the church at Corinth how the temptations that felled their fathers were gospel issues. The Israelites, after all, probably saw their "issues" as relatively mundane—water management, food supply, leadership struggles, and so on. But more was at work. They all drank "spiritual" water from a "spiritual" Rock, Paul said (1 Cor. 10:3–4). Now this wouldn't have seemed "spiritual" to the Israelites. It was just a rock, and it was just water. We tend to think "spiritual" means ghostly or otherworldly religious. This was just a normal part of life, it seemed. But the Spirit was the One giving it. And that "Rock," Paul said, "was Christ" (1 Cor. 10:4). When they rebelled against the Spirit's provision, they were really rebelling against God's purposes and order, the One in whom all God's promises find their "Yes" and their "Amen" (2 Cor. 1:20).

The Corinthian believers had a hard time seeing how their particular temptations—factions, tolerance of sexual immorality, eating food offered to idols, disorder at the Lord's Table, debates over the bodily resurrection—had anything do with the larger questions of Christian identity. In every case, the apostle framed their temptations as gospel matters. The same is true for all of us.

Gospel freedom is the most important aspect of resisting temptation. Remember that Satan's power over you is first and foremost the power of accusation and threatened death. In Christ, though, you have already been indicted, judged, executed, and resurrected. You are "dead to sin and alive to God in Christ Jesus" (Rom. 6:11). Regardless of whether you support or oppose the death penalty, you'd probably wince to hear about a state that executed a murderer and then had a public flogging of his corpse. Your discomfort there wouldn't be because you're soft on murder but because that act would be insanely beside the point. After all, an executed corpse can't be punished anymore. It's over.

Likewise, you've been to hell, in the cross of Christ. You've been buried beneath the judgment of God, turned over to the Devil, and you are gone. Now you stand in Christ, hidden in his identity, and thus free from any accusation. Knowing that truth doesn't lead you to yield to temptation but instead to fly from it. You're not hiding from God anymore.

Jesus overcame temptation because he consistently believed God's Word about him—"You are my beloved Son"—even when he walked in the wild places. Because there was no sin in him, his communion with his Father was unbroken. The gospel reminds you continually that you are found in Christ, that the Christ-life is being lived out in you through the Spirit, and that the Father is therefore pleased with you. The more you look to Christ, the less you hide.

One of the first ways you can tell that you are moving beyond temptation into a pattern of sin is if you find yourself in a time of prayerlessness. That isn't just a "spiritual maturity issue"—it's a gospel issue. You are recreated through the gospel with a nature that longs for communion with God. The Spirit within you cries out, "Abba! Father!" (Rom. 8:15; Gal. 4:6). Prayer is exactly how you experience the sympathy of your High Priest who has triumphed over your temptation. After all, you are not the only one praying when you pray. The Spirit himself prays through you, and as he does so, he works to align your will and desires with those of Christ Jesus (Rom. 8:26–27). If you are reluctant to pray, it just might be that you, like Adam and Israel before you, are hiding in the vegetation, ashamed to hear the rustling of the leaves that signals he is here.

Some of you may be genuinely unsure of whether you've ever trusted in the gospel in the first place, and maybe for good reason. Perhaps you've never really repented of sin, or perhaps you've never really seen the glory of Christ. If so, repent and believe. But many more of you are probably facing a lack of assurance of salvation not because the Spirit is absent from your life but because he is present. My friend Felix thought he couldn't possibly be a Christian because he was in agony over temptation and sin. But that's the very definition of a Christian this side of the resurrection. It is an unbeliever, not a believer, who is untroubled and tranquil in his rebellion.

The Spirit, though, is at work in making us into who we are in Christ, and that's momentarily painful. The demonic powers have an interest in keeping you under a lack of assurance of your acceptance by God. If you fear that you are under judgment, you will slink back away from God, into the darkness.

Your prayerlessness will lead you to cover over your sin, and your cover-up will lead to more sin.

When I was a child, I would occasionally visit some relatives' home in another town. The kids my age there didn't do much exploring in the woods like my friends and I back home liked to do. They were really hard-core religious, and they didn't have a television. What they did have, though, were fundamentalist Christian comic books, and they were fascinating. They were as dark and conspiratorial as the pulpy fantasy magazines we weren't allowed to read, except with a gospel invitation at the back. Mostly they just passed the time away, but one of them scared me to death.

This little cartoon tract showed a dead man on Judgment Day. The figure of God in there wasn't particularly scary, just a white-robed man with a blank face (I'm not talking about expression; literally blank, no facial features at all) with squiggly lines drawn out from his head (rays of glory, I guess).

What was terrifying, though, was what the tract said happened to this guy. He was shown a film, in front of God and everybody (and I do mean everybody; his friends and neighbors and biblical characters were all there), of all the secret sins he'd done in life. The dead man character would squirm and sweat and gnash his teeth in embarrassment, but he couldn't deny anything. It was all there, on this screen. "This was your life," a fierce-looking angel announced.

I thought about that comic book a lot, and it terrorized me. What would my parents think when they found out about some of the things I'd done? What would my Sunday school teacher do when she saw what I was thinking about while she was teaching us insipid songs about Noah and his "arky-arky" made of "gopher barky barky"? The very idea made me cringe.

Now the comic book—like others in that series—might have been a bit overdone and lacking in nuance. But my fear in the face of it was the normal human condition. This amateurish cartoon exposed what I intuitively knew to be true—"no creature is hidden from [God's] sight, but all are naked and exposed to the eyes of him to whom we must give account" (Heb. 4:13). I hadn't done much, comparatively speaking, but I'd done enough to make me feel wild and to experience the sensation of "fight or flight" before my "fearful expectation of judgment" (Heb. 10:27).

I've outgrown that comic book, of course, but I still find exposure to be alienating. Maybe you do too. Think about it for a moment. What in your life would you fear if anyone found out about it? What would horrify you if it were exposed before your family, your friends, your acquaintances?

In gospel repentance and faith, we fearlessly expose ourselves to Judgment Day in the present. That's what the confession of sin is, a revealing of what Jesus already promises to reveal on the Day of Christ (Luke 8:17). Our problem is that we often, like Adam before us, want to hide our temptations, and especially our sin—to cover it over to save face. Hiding, though, is exactly the opposite of what a Christian does when confronted with satanic designs. The darkness is where these evils latch onto us. Instead we can preemptively shine light on this, with God in prayer and in our authentic accountability to the Body of Christ, his church.

Our Christian reluctance to speak honestly about temptation is precisely why Christians like Felix often believe themselves to be unbelievers. All they see of other believers is this façade of smiling, peaceful Christ-followers. They assume then that the internal life of every other Christian is just a continual festival of hymns as opposed to their own internal life, in which the hymns are interrupted with constant gossipy chatter, violent rage, and hard-core pornography. This is exactly how the satanic powers want it. They want the prideful and oblivious to stay that way until they fall and slink away in isolation, where they can be devoured. Preaching the gospel to ourselves, though, reminds us continually that we are sinners and that we can stand only by the blood of Jesus. We can walk only by his Spirit prodding us on. We need one another, as parts of the same body together.

Often our pride not only keeps us from not seeing our points of vulnerability but also keeps us from opening ourselves to exposure to others in the body of Christ. The Scripture says that we are to "bear one another's burdens" and that the stronger in the faith should restore the weaker "in a spirit of gentleness" (Gal. 6:1–2). We often do exactly the reverse. Those who are weak, perhaps grappling with some temptation, don't feel able to speak to the spiritually strong. Instead they can find empathy only with those who are weak in the same points.

That's why our church "accountability groups" for those facing some particular temptation are often filled with those tempted at the same point. To some degree this is wise. One battling an eating disorder, for instance, can often be helped greatly by one who has already overcome this, and the same might be true of some sexual compulsion or marital disharmony or anger or whatever it might be. But the weak need the strong, and the strong need the weak in order to be reminded of their own points of weakness, especially when they are temporarily submerged.

The self-humbling spirit of Christ that comes to us in our initial act of repentance, signified in our baptism in Christ, manifests itself throughout the Christian life as we confess that we need one another. We don't then hide our temptations from one another but expose them to the light of mutual accountability and scrutiny. In my own case, most often I keep temptations and sins covered over because of pride. I don't want to be thought of as someone who is weak in some particular point, and I'm fearful of what someone might think of me if I confess that I fear I don't have the resources to combat something that's stalking me.

But that kind of isolating pride is countergospel. We've been crucified with Christ. We are already humiliated. In Jesus, our corpses were hanging in the sun, publicly marking us out as sinners worthy of death. If we are repentant, we are always clinging to the fact that we agree with God's just judgment against us. What then is there left to hide?

The first step in fighting temptation is to remember who you are in Christ and to situate that within a larger story of God's kingdom economy, the economy of the gospel. This means reading the Bible the way Jesus reads it, not the way the Devil preaches it. Apart from Christ, there simply are no promises of God. In his temptation of Jesus, Satan quoted Scripture, and he didn't, remember, misquote anything. God wants his children to eat bread, not to starve before stones. God will protect his anointed one with the angels of heaven. God will give his Messiah all the kingdoms of the earth. All this is true. What is satanic about all of this, though, is that Satan wanted our Lord to grasp these things apart from the cross and the empty tomb. But these promises couldn't be abstracted from the gospel without becoming devilish to the core.

You can go to hell believing Bible verses abstracted from Jesus. You can read the message of Psalm 24: "Who shall ascend the hill of the LORD? And who shall stand in his holy place? He who has clean hands and a pure heart, who does not lift up his soul to what is false and does not swear deceitfully" (vv. 3–4). Perhaps the Pharisee that Jesus mentioned had this verse in mind when he stood in the temple, right next to the repentant tax-swindler. "Thank you, God, that I can approach you with clean hands and a pure heart," he might have said. And his successors say it still, including some in the pews of some of our most faithful churches. That attitude is damning.

It's not damning because the psalm is untrue. It is truth. It is damning because there is only one Man with a pure heart and clean hands, only One who is the righteousness of God. If I pretend to come to God apart from him, as though this text or any other applies to me outside of Jesus Christ, I will only find condemnation. But hidden in Christ, this promise is my promise. When I cry out with the sinful tax collector, "Have mercy!" and find myself in Christ, then everything God has promised to Jesus now belongs to me.

Think through whatever it is that's tempting you right now. Ask God for wisdom, for him to open up your mind to see things as they are. Then talk to someone in your life, a more mature believer or a group of believers in your church. Take the mystery away from whatever's tempting you, regardless of how embarrassing it is. Don't spin it into something more acceptable. Don't worry about how pathetic it makes you look. If you're tempted to sin against your spouse, tell your spouse what's tempting you. Bring it into the light. And then pray (this one is hard) that God would expose your sin. By nature you're going to want to hide beneath a façade. The gospel exposes you as a sinner, and the gospel embraces you as a son or daughter. Claim your new identity, and don't fight the Spirit as he seeks to crucify the old one.

REORDERING YOUR DESIRES

Felix told me he'd been working out frenetically at a gym just to exhaust himself at night so that he wouldn't have the energy to think about what he'd been thinking about. That didn't work. The more we talked about it, though, the clearer what Felix was expecting became. It wasn't just triumph over sin he wanted. He wanted an end to the temptation. For him, sanctification means a kind of inner tranquillity in which he doesn't want what he doesn't want to want. I could relate. But the gospel doesn't promise us any such thing.

The word "struggle" has become a cliché, especially in evangelical Christian circles. It's a way to place a kind of distance between my rebellion and myself. There's a big difference between saying to my fellow believers that I "struggle with procrastination" and confessing "I'm lazy." But grappling with temptation is torturous. It's not for nothing that the Scripture often compares this grappling to physical violence—cutting off a limb or poking out an eye (Matt. 5:29–30), having one's skin set afire (Mark 9:49; 1 Cor. 7:9), or fighting until one is bleeding all over the place (Heb. 12:4). This is because our desires are so strong.

The apostle Paul placed the pull to temptation in the context of human desires, showing how the Israelites of old moved from eating and drinking to outright rebellion and debauchery (1 Cor. 10:7). Again, at this point the Scripture keeps us away from both hubris and despair. The Scripture tells us we'll encounter temptation, and that it will be wild. The Bible also tells us that we must resist temptation. As a matter of fact, the Word of God promises us that if we'll fight the temptation, we'll win. "Resist the devil, and he will flee from you" (James 4:7). Notice that all that is necessary is the resistance. When you resist the temptation, the Spirit handles the rest.

Some of you probably feel your particular temptation is kind of freakish, and ultimately irresistible. You're wrong. The Scripture tells us that there is no temptation that isn't "common to man" (1 Cor. 10:13). Now this doesn't mean that we all want the exact same things. Just since I've been writing this book I was told of a man who was arrested for walking nude through a women's gymnasium wearing nothing but sunglasses. I can't understand much about this. "What is so thrilling about that?" I asked a friend. "And why the sunglasses?" I'm sure there are temptations I have that would be no struggle for you at all. The point, though, is that the temptations we face are all personality-specific variations of those universally common entry points for sin, the places where our Lord Jesus was tempted in the desert. No matter what it is that you're struggling against, you are a sinner, but you are not a freak.

Moreover, don't fall for the illusion that the strength of your desire means that your temptations are irresistible. This is not the case. "God is faithful," Paul wrote, "and he will not let you be tempted beyond your ability, but with the temptation he will also provide the way of escape, that you may be able to endure it" (1 Cor. 10:13).

Do you see the freedom in that? The satanic powers are at play with the temptations around you; but, just as with Job, God is ultimately sovereign even over the dark spirits. He says to them, "This far and no farther," and he bases that on what your physical, spiritual, and psychological frame can endure.

Moreover, in the middle of any temptation he has crafted a way for you to escape from it.

The Spirit, through the gospel, connects us with the life of Jesus, making us like him. Part of what that means is that we learn to discipline ourselves—to redirect our desires and to cultivate those desires that flow from his life. The fruit of the Sprit, then, includes self-control. You might read the subheading of this chapter and mumble to yourself, "But I can't resist temptation—I don't have reordered desires; my desires are just as out of kilter as they were the day I came to know Christ." But you're not seeing the whole picture. Stop thinking of yourself as an isolated individual, and start seeing yourself as the gospel does, as part of a head/body unity between Christ and his church. Jesus' desires are ordered toward the will of God. As the head, he is restoring his whole body, his church, to the same direction. Right now this is kind of like a stroke victim going through physical therapy. You are a toe that is learning again how to respond to the stimuli from the head. If you are in Christ, your desires will line up with his eventually. Count on it (Rom. 8:29).

Resistance to temptation means taking desire seriously. Both Jesus and Satan do. There is a way to seek to coach people toward "victory" over their desires simply by downplaying how powerful those desires actually are. It is the message of, "Just don't do it." For a while that makes perfect sense. It makes sense (it has, in fact, the "appearance of wisdom") to say of those things that might awaken the lusts of the flesh, "Do not handle, Do not taste, Do not touch." But such restrictions "are of no value in stopping the indulgence of the flesh" (Col. 2:21, 23).

Why? Because the desires are made to be stronger than human decisions. They are meant to show you that you are a creature and to point you to Christ. The antidote is to see where those desires point to the gospel and to cling to the mystery itself, or rather to the mystery himself. That doesn't mean, though, that the answer is just to "believe" more doctrinal systems or have more "spiritual" experiences (although both doctrine and piety are essential to Christian discipleship).

The Scripture doesn't downplay the pull of the desires. It honestly acknowledges them, which is precisely why God speaks to the proper use of every appetite—from that for food, to that of sex, to that of sleep, and on and on. A too carnal view of desire is devilish. That's the case whether the carnality is in normalizing and surrendering to the desires or whether the carnality is in thinking that desires can be governed merely with external rules. But a too spiritual view of the passions is also devilish, a view that doesn't see how primal and powerful those desires are designed to be. Don't have sex, we tell our teenagers and young adults. But two teenagers in a sleeping bag together are going to have sex—unless one of them is the reincarnation of Joan of Arc or one of them is castrated. Human beings weren't designed to have that kind of willpower in that kind of situation.

A lack of specificity, with one another and to ourselves, often fuels temptation. If we simply say, "Don't be greedy," the slumlord will simply define *greedy* as whatever Wall Street tycoons do. If we say, "Be chaste," the young adult will believe he's sexually pure because he's only had oral sex. If we simply say, "Be content," the family will assume they're content even as they claw ahead to pile up all the advertised stuff in their rented, climate-controlled storage units. Specificity exposes how the designs of Satan mask themselves.

You might rattle on about "the family" while neglecting your children. You might fight for "social justice" by "raising consciousness" about "the poor," while judging your friends by how trendy their clothes are. You might pontificate about "the church" while not knowing the names of the people in the seats around you in your local congregation. Abstraction distances.

"The family" never shows up unexpectedly for Thanksgiving or criticizes your spouse or spills chocolate milk all over your carpet; only real families can do that. "The poor" don't show up drunk for the job interview you've scheduled or spend the money you've given them on lottery tickets or tell you they hate you; only real people can do that. "The church" never votes down your position in a congregational business meeting or puts on an embarrassingly bad Easter musical or asks you to clean toilets before children's camp next week; only real churches can do that. As long as "the family" or "the poor" or "the church" are abstract concepts, they can be whoever I want them to be. The same is true with temptation and sin.

The Spirit warns us about this. King David knew adultery was wrong; but he didn't want *anyone* meddling with his situation with Bathsheba. Jesus lit into the Pharisees for "fighting for" the Law of God while ignoring their financial obligations to their parents, all under the guise of religious advocacy (Mark 7:10–13). Specificity identifies where, particularly, temptation (and post-temptation sin) is afoot.

At the same time, though, too much specificity—in the form of mere external rules and regulations—doesn't stifle desires but rather redirects and inflames them. It's true that it is easier just to cordon off certain areas, for fear of falling into them. The apostle Paul could have saved much space in the New Testament on the ethics of eating meat offered to idols simply by commanding the churches to be vegetarian. Much of the dialogue we currently have about how much is "enough" and how much is "too much" for Christians would have been solved if Jesus had given us a maximum yearly income—adjusted for inflation and the exchange rate between our currency and Roman denarii. But the Spirit doesn't do this.

That's because, for one thing, the satanic schemes are too crafty for this. Legalism doesn't just make us miserable. Legalism damns us to hell as we navigate around the rules to wherever our appetite lies hidden, ready to feed us till we want no more. Some of the most rigid religious schools, for example, also turn out to be the most hedonistic. The students there are subjected to rule after rule about length of hair and what music they can to listen to and what time to go to bed; men and women are put on different sidewalks in order to keep them from temptation. The rules are so hyperscrupulous that one can't help but break them. And in so doing, one learns to defy the authority.

Before long the authority itself is seen as arbitrary. Like children with an overbearing father, the students conclude they can never meet these expectations and give up trying. They learn to justify the rule breaking by smuggling in "secular" music or reading with a flashlight after lights out. They learn how to mimic external conformity in public and to flout it in private. They don't wear immodest clothes or drink beers, but they're pulling each other's zippers down in the backseat of a parked car three miles away from campus—maybe even with some of that forbidden "secular" music playing in the background.

Now certain areas are temptations for anyone, and all Christians should avoid them. This isn't legalism. But there are many areas in which our weak points don't coincide and in which we could never predict what would destroy a brother or sister for whom Christ died.

One person is vulnerable to temptation by eating meat; so he shouldn't eat it (Rom. 14:2–3). Another person is vulnerable to alcoholism; maybe she shouldn't eat in a restaurant that serves it. One person is incited to lust by underwear advertisements, so she avoids the mall; another recognizes that certain dinner parties tempt him to gossip, so he goes running instead. Because the temptations are person specific, often the resistance to them is the same. The answer is balance and gratitude and knowing one another in community well enough to encourage one another toward the good and away from evil (Gal. 6:1–2).

Sanctification isn't usually rapid (at least as we count time). The drive for self-control then is often piecemeal. It could be that whatever tempts you is simply too "big" for you to contemplate as a whole. If so, then hack away at individual bits of it. For instance, you might be tempted toward a fearfulness of what other people think of you. It's probably not doable to commit to "stop being fearful." What you could do, however, is to start with something small—say, working up the courage to give your testimony in your church small group. The victory that you, through the Spirit, achieve there can give you the war map for further taking on this issue in your life. You probably can't contemplate how to "stop being lazy," but you can start getting out of bed fifteen minutes earlier each day, learning the discipline to deny yourself what you crave in order to train yourself for godliness.

Ultimately, though, the answer to reshaping your desires is to be in communion with God through the gospel, through the renewing of your mind, as the apostle Paul puts it (Rom. 12:2). The "mind" in Scripture is not chiefly your cognitive capacity, as though storing up memorized Bible verses for the purpose of information could stave off temptation. It is instead the core of your ability to perceive. That is intellectual, yes, to some degree, but also intuitive, personal, emotional, imaginative. Know the Scripture, but know the Scripture as Jesus knows the Scripture, with the gospel of Christ at the center and with the worship of the triune God as the focus. This means the cultivation not just of knowledge as we typically think of it but also of imagination, just as Paul did in carrying the Corinthians back to the scene of their ancestors' crimes.

As the writer David Mills argues, rightly, contemporary Christianity errs when it deemphasizes the stories of the faith in favor of the abstracted principles or doctrines mined from them. "Revulsion is a much better protection from the force of the passions than an intellectual understanding by itself," Mills writes. "To feel 'This is yucky' is not a final protection from sin, but it is better than thinking 'This is wrong' but feeling 'This is okay.'"[2] The same is true in the reverse positive sense. It is infinitely better to feel the weight of glory in the Scriptures, to know the contours of the shape of Scripture even if you don't know your way to the specific chapters and verses, than to have detailed memorization of Scripture as a cognitive category. There are some, I fear, who will be able to diagram in Greek the last words they ever hear voiced: "Depart from me, you worker of iniquity." Such cognitive expertise is of little use in wrestling demons.

This means saturation in the Scripture as you pray through it, rather than tracking down all the Bible verses you need to confront whatever sin you're facing at the moment. Jesus didn't study Deuteronomy 6 and 8 in order to fight the Devil in the desert. They were just there, embedded in his moral imagination. And when he heard the offers of the demon, they didn't ring true to the better voice he'd heard in the ancient writings. God knows what you will need to fight your present and future temptations. You'll find it uncanny how words will shape you and how the Spirit will give you strength to stand by those words.

The gospel calls us to listen to the Spirit—in Scripture and through God's forming of us through his providential discipline. As you read the Scripture, ask God to discern your heart and to discipline you. When you read the words, "Blessed is the man who walks not in the counsel of the wicked" (Ps. 1:1), you could pray, "Lord, expose for me the ways I listen to wicked counsel." When you read, "Blessed are the meek, for they shall inherit the earth" (Matt. 5:5), you could pray, "God, would you please actively oppose every haughty thing I try in order to keep it from succeeding." Beg the Lord to show you what you don't see, and what you don't want to see. Solomon asked for wisdom, and he received it because he was God's anointed. You are too—if you are in Christ. That's exactly why James exhorts us to ask for wisdom when we lack it (James 1:5).

Most of all, as you seek maturity, wisdom, and self-control to discipline your desires, to line them up with those of Christ Jesus, don't expect the struggle to end. You will not ever enter a time of being spared temptation until you experience your head pushing upward through the dirt in front of a gravestone with your name on it. Until that day of resurrection, there will be a skirmish. You will triumph over specific temptations, yes, but they'll be back. Sometimes your desire for some temptation will completely evaporate. You might know the heroin addict, for instance, who never wants the drug again. But that's quite rare. Most of us will constantly scrap against the same persistent temptations. And even when those temptations leave, others will replace them, often nastier and more deadly than the first.

This is the part that is scary for most people. We're able to identify with the little boy dreaming about "wild things" because it seems as though they just can't be tamed. When the temper tantrums move from outside to inside, it frightens you. When you have a sexual fantasy while sitting in church, it alarms you. You wonder whether the fight you're putting up is as futile as rock-throwing children taking on a nuclear power. But you're not seeing your own struggle, or the larger cosmic fabric, very clearly. You have "not yet," as the Scripture puts it, "resisted to the point of shedding your blood" (Heb. 12:4).

Moreover, you know you can overcome whatever you're grappling against. Sure, you may have a genetic basis for that alcoholic craving or that sexual urge or that fiery temper. But the fact that you have it means that God designed you, knowing you could follow Christ even with that thorn in your flesh or psyche (1 Cor. 10:13). As you face the temptation, know that God is walking you through it, just as surely as the Spirit led our Lord Jesus in and out of his desert testing. The temptation itself ought to be a revelation to you. God is saying, "You have been created and gifted with the ability to walk away from this."

The problem is, though, that we often think escape from temptation, promised by God, means escape from the agony of struggling against temptation, which it does not. Don't pray for an end to the struggle. Pray for your warfare to be more effective as you dodge fiery darts on the way into the kingdom. Peace is a fruit of the Spirit, but that's peace with God and with one another. It is emphatically not peace with the world, the flesh, and the Devil. That's why the Bible can include such a seemingly discordant statement about peace as "The God of peace will soon crush Satan under your feet" (Rom. 16:20). Don't be discouraged or depressed if you're in agony fighting against your temptations. That means the Holy Spirit is there. And where the Spirit is, for now anyway, there is war (Gal. 5:17).

REFRAMING YOUR FUTURE

Several years ago Jessica, a new Christian, found her father hanging from a rope in her room, dead by his own hand. She was haunted by this horror, of course, and even more so because it was obvious he had planned to be found in a place where she'd be the one to find him. In the suicide note, he criticized and taunted Jessica, calling her a disappointment and a failure.

For years she didn't want to fall in love, didn't want to marry, because she knew her destiny. Her father wasn't alone in killing himself. His father had done the same, as had his father before him. There was something dark in the gene pool back there, she thought, and she saw the same depressive tendencies in herself that her father had at that age. She could see her future before her, and in it she was hanging from a rope. She just didn't want any children there to suffer for another generation as she had through hers.

Now you might not have something as horrific as all of that behind you and in front of you. But there's something there. And many of us often feel as helpless as Jessica when surveying our past patterns and our future prospects. But Jessica is wrong in the way she's seeing this—and so are you. You are not your history, and you are not your destiny. If you are in Christ, you are a new creation. Your past is his past, and your future is his future. You do not have to be what you are.

In one sense Jessica is actually gifted with a perception many of us can't see (or simply ignore). She has looked at the possible outcome of her life if she follows a particular path. If she embraces this as a Christian, it could actually prove to be a way to empower her resistance to temptation.

The apostle Paul warned the church at Corinth about the consequences of sin by pointing them to a picture of an alternative reality, to what would happen if they fell to Satan's strategies. The Israelite ancestors, Paul wrote, were "destroyed by serpents" and "destroyed by the Destroyer" (1 Cor. 10:9–10). Twenty-three thousand of them fell "in a single day" (1 Cor. 10:8). They were "overthrown in the wilderness" (1 Cor. 10:5). This, Paul wrote, is an "example" for us (1 Cor. 10:11). Again, these were clearly believers in the church at Corinth. But the apostle nonetheless thought they ought to know about the disaster that could await them, a theme consistent throughout the Bible. God uses warnings to keep us from falling.

As you face whatever temptation you're up against, consider the warning of temporal disaster. The simple truth is that when you're in the throes of giving in to a temptation, you just don't know what you really want. The bread that was previously stone might taste good, but Jesus knew it wasn't worth being excluded from the table of God. God has designed the universe in such a way that we flourish when we walk with the grain of the cosmos and not against it. Taking a dog by the ears might seem to be an exciting thing to do in the moment, but observation of human nature and of dog nature and of the way the world works ought to keep you from doing it (Prov. 26:17).

In the book of Proverbs a father showed his son the inevitable results of adultery. These aren't only the eschatological results (those that we can know by faith) but also those that can be observed, over the period of a life, by sight. The bitter end of this momentary ecstasy is disgrace and ruin (Prov. 5:8–14). In his providential discipline of us, God tends to put such pictures before us, that we might watch and take warning. A while back I heard of a pastor I'd long respected who was caught in a secret pattern of sin. What seared into my conscience wasn't his sin (which wasn't all that unusual) or even the loss of his ministry, his reputation, and his home. What I remember most is hearing him talk about what it was like to drive several hours away to his daughter's college dormitory room to tell her what her dad had done. I don't even have a daughter, and my children are far from college-aged, but I could envision that scenario, with horror. The human carnage of that struck me, and haunts me even now. Often in moments like this, what you hear is the Spirit saying, "This easily could be you. Hear and be warned."

This is one of the reasons we need an intimacy between generations in our families and in our churches. These days most people spend a large portion of their lives staring at screens and "consuming media." Previous generations would have ended their evenings gathered around listening to one another tell stories or sing ballads or recite sagas. There is something lost there. When all I have is my peer group and the "entertainment" marketed to my peer group, I lose the kind of perspective that sees the ultimate comeuppance of pride or the heartbreak of sexual licentiousness or the sadness of dying with nothing more than a bunch of stuff piled around you.

Moreover, we're all going to face the unique temptations that come with each stage of life. We teach our children ahead of time that puberty will mean that "a lot of strange things will be happening." Why don't we do the same thing in having older men preparing thirtysomethings for the testosterone drop that often prompts a so-called "midlife crisis"? Why can't older women teach younger women how to handle the hormonal upheaval that can come with menopause and how to go through it with Christlikeness? Why couldn't the elderly in our congregations warn the younger generations about the pull toward bitterness or despondency or rage that can come with failing health or life in nursing homes?

As you resist temptation, keep a close watch on the stories around you, not with a prurient interest and certainly not with a sense of moral superiority, but with a sense of warned empathy. You could be in every one of those situations. Feel the horror that comes with each of them.

Also, though, keep before your conscience the warnings of eternal loss. I recognize that this section will probably trouble many of you, so let me preface it by saying what I'm not arguing. I am not arguing that you ought to be wondering whether or not Jesus will reject you and you'll go to hell. I believe one who is genuinely born from above by the Spirit will continue in that faith until the very end. The one who believes in Christ will be raised with him at the last day (John 6:40). But at the same time no one will be saved who doesn't "endure to the end" (Matt. 10:22; 24:13; Mark 13:13). The Spirit ensures that the living faith that begins at the onset of the Christian life continues throughout it.

And the Spirit uses warnings, as well as promises, in order to prod us along to continued faith and repentance.[3] If I'm tempted to deny Jesus in the face of persecution, the Spirit prompts me to remember that "whoever denies me before men, I also will deny before my Father who is in heaven" (Matt. 10:33). When I am tempted to refuse to forgive, the Spirit prompts me to consider that "if you do not forgive others their trespasses, neither will your Father forgive your trespasses" (Matt. 6:15). This needn't create a lack of assurance. The apostle Paul, after all, knew with complete certainty that he was saved; he had seen the Lord Jesus and heard his voice telling him so (Acts 9:1–19). Nonetheless, Paul wrote to the tempted Corinthians, about himself, "But I discipline my body and keep it under control, lest after preaching to others I myself should be disqualified" (1 Cor. 9:27). The gravity of hell before us doesn't rob us of assurance but actually propels us toward it because it creates repentance. Repentance, and confession of sin, are the means by which our consciences are cleansed (1 John 1:9).

More important than the warnings are the promises. God knows, in the short term and in the eternal term, what it takes to give us the peace, wholeness, and life that we crave. If the immediate is all you see, you are going to be unable to see the joy that comes, for example, with being able to hold your dementia-ridden spouse's hand knowing you never violated your marriage covenant. It is not easy to see the kind of joy that comes with ending a "small" but good life as opposed to having a powerful but miserable one. You don't know what's best for you. You don't even know what you really want. Sometimes what we want is hell. Your Father knows what's best for you, and he'll train your affections until you want it too.

And even greater than temporal blessing, which is often difficult to see through finite sinful eyes, is the "assurance of things hoped for, the conviction of things not seen" (Heb. 11:1). Part of this is because it's simply impossible for us to comprehend such glory right now (1 Cor. 2:9). Also, we learn to hope for what we don't yet perceive because God knows that produces the patience that yields the character we'll need to rule as kings and queens over his creation (Rom. 8:18–23; 1 Pet. 1:4–9; 2 Pet. 1:5–11). This emerging patience is a sign that we are becoming "partakers of the divine nature" (2 Pet. 1:4), right along with our Lord Jesus. Finally, we're able to see why our promise is delayed when we see ourselves in the context of the whole church, that number no man can number streaming through the millennia "awesome as an army with banners" (Song 6:10).

Clinging to the promises of God, again, isn't primarily an intellectual activity. It is first and foremost a receiving of glory, a glory that is perceived by more than just the cognitive capacity. The prophet Isaiah was undone by the light of the glory of God's presence (Isa. 6:1–6). The apostle John tells us that the glory Isaiah saw was Jesus of Nazareth (John 12:41). When we hear the gospel preached and when we worship through Jesus together, the glory of God breaks through (2 Cor. 4:6). Some people recoil at that light; some people run to it (John 3:19–21).

Sometimes the most effective thing you can do to combat temptation is to leave your accountability group for a while and sense a foretaste of the New Jerusalem with your local congregation, singing hymns and songs, eating bread and drinking wine, and hearing the voice of Jesus through the preached Word. As you do so, remember you're part of a transnational, trans-generational, trans-ethnic body of the redeemed. Those singing with you in heaven right now have already been through your struggles. That cloud of witnesses gathers around you, spurring you on in hope. Those around you are likewise groaning for the same redemption for which you long. And before all of you stands Jesus—who was tempted, tested, tortured, and yet is, finally, triumphant. As you perceive his invisible glory, you begin to see what seemed incredible in the wilderness. You will find that you'll be able to say, as did writer Flannery O'Connor: "I believe love to be efficacious in the loooong run."[4]

CONCLUSION

When I read to my sons about the "wild things," they always seem to calm down at the very end. The "wild rumpus" quiets down when the book puts the rambunctious young hero back in his room after his journey is over. It's the same room his mother had sent him off to, for his wildness, without his supper. But now, after his time with the wild things, he finds his supper waiting for him in his room. "And it was still hot," the book concludes.

At the time this book was published, the eminent psychiatrist Bruno Bettelheim said the scary nature of the story was found in the "time out" in the room itself. "The basic anxiety of the child is desertion," Bettelheim said. "To be sent to bed alone is one desertion, and without food is the second desertion. The combination is the worst desertion that can threaten a child."[5] I'm not sure whether the psychiatrist has read the story correctly, but I am sure that we're all, and not just children, fearful at some level of desertion. And that's exactly why the temptations of Jesus carry such a primal note of liberation and freedom for all of us. It's hard to imagine a scene that seems more like desertion than starving in a desert. But even there Jesus was not deserted by the Father. And neither are we.

Temptation seems irresistible because our affections haven't yet been trained fully for the glory that awaits us. Moreover, temptation often prods us right into sin because we haven't yet learned fully to believe that "God is faithful" to provide a "way of escape" from our wildness (1 Cor. 10:13). Like children frightened by the wild things, we retreat backward into "the spirit of slavery" and so "fall back into fear" (Rom. 8:15). The gospel, though, reminds us, all life long, that we have one who has gone ahead "as a forerunner on our behalf" (Heb. 6:20). We hear therefore a voice telling us to "be strong and courageous," for "I will not leave you or forsake you" (Josh. 1:5), no matter how wild you feel inside. He's the only one with the authority to tell the Devil to "be gone."

In my nightly Bible readings with my family, I read a selected narrative in the canon, but every night my children beg me to read "the one about the snake." For some reason they love to hear about Moses combating the fiery serpents in the wilderness with the bronze serpent on the pole and about the afflicted finding healing when they look at the emblem of the very curse that's killing them. My little boys don't simply have a morbid fascination with venomous snakes among the wandering Israelites. In fact, they are never satisfied to end the story there.

They wait in silence until we turn to what they call "the other pole," the picture of the cross of Christ. That's when I tell them how mysteriously this seemingly helpless, executed man confronted the snake of Eden right there on "the other pole" and finally did what God had promised since the beginning of history. He crushed its head. He went out beyond the gates of Jerusalem to "where the wild things are"—and he conquered wildness forever. They seem to sleep better hearing that.

And so do I.

7

(NOT A) CONCLUSION

If you're going to commit a sin, a church baptistery is an awfully awkward place to do it. And five minutes before you're publicly identified with Jesus Christ is a fairly awkward time to do it too. But honestly, at the time, I was cheering him on, and I was the preacher.

This new convert and I were standing in a hallway behind the platform at my church, just steps away from wading down into the baptismal pool where I would enact the ancient church rite marking him out as our brother in Christ. He was twisting the ring on his left hand, rubbing the back of his hair every few seconds, and walking over to the garbage can to spit.

Part of it, I think, was that he really wanted a cigarette. Part of it was that this was all new to him. I don't think he even knew, yet, the difference between what the big numbers and the little numbers mean in his Bible, let alone the difference between the red letters and the black. From what he'd told me there had been lots of manic sex, empty pill bottles, and stale marijuana smoke back there in the past he was putting behind him. He'd been lots of places, but he'd never planned to be here.

I showed him the water and reassured him it wasn't too cold, that I wouldn't hold him under too long, and all the other things that tend to make people nervous. I told him everything that would happen in a few minutes, when we went out into the water in front of his excited new church family. I could tell from the way he smiled and wiped away tears that he was thrilled. I could also tell from the way he kept looking at the side door that he hadn't completely ruled out bolting from the place.

I told him that I would ask three questions there in the water in front of the watching congregation. The first was, "Do you confess with your mouth Jesus as Lord?" He nodded his head. "Do you believe in your heart that God has raised him from the dead?" Again he nodded. "Do you renounce the Devil and all his works?" He jerked his face forward and yelled, "Oh my God!"

I winced, but not because I was offended. This is a fairly common saying in contemporary American culture. I don't usually mind what people say around me, especially not unbelievers and new believers, and especially not something as relatively mild at that. I was just afraid the elderly couple standing with us, there to help with any last-minute details, might rebuke him for "taking the Lord's name in vain." They had already exchanged harried glances with each other the time he had used the adjective "freaking." I was just glad that's what he'd said, because I could tell it was a very recently acquired euphemism.

What mattered, though, wasn't so much what he said as what must have been whirring through his mind. He didn't find it incredible that I was asking him to affirm that a two thousand-year-old ex-corpse would now be his slave master for life. He'd already grappled with that when he heard the claims of the gospel and believed them. He was just stunned to hear me say that about the Devil. It wasn't that he found it crazy (well, maybe a little). It was that he found it creepy. He'd never thought about Satan in such personal, such confrontational terms. It was as though he had walked into another dimension, one in which dripping wet people incited fights with demons.

That's because he had.

As I walked him up the stairs to the baptistery and waited for the choir music to end so we could step out into the water,

I thought about what he'd be up against soon. He'd doubt, at some point, whether or not all this is real, whether his guilt is really gone, really washed away by someone else's blood. He'd feel pulled back to some of the old patterns he used to know, and it would be torturous to say no. The clarity with which he saw eternity right now—both the judgment from which he was fleeing and the kingdom toward which he was running—would diminish, and the everyday things would seem much more pressing, much more real.

The more I thought about his exclamation, the more convicted I felt. You see, I'd been working on writing this book, and I'd spent a lot of time thinking through satanic strategies and the Christian counterstrategies to hold back temptation. But through it all I kept eluding the main point.

I hope now that you've finished this book (unless you're one of those folks who start books at the end and read backwards), you have a little more perception of what's going on in the skirmish for your life. I hope you recognize the satanic offers that come to you for self-directed provision or protection or exaltation. I hope you see how our Lord Jesus can intercede for you, how the Spirit can fight through you. But mostly I hope you see the point of it all. You cannot triumph over temptation. Only Jesus can.

What I often want is a surefire way to stop the temptation. I could get a lot more done with my life. What I'm really wanting is to set myself up as wiser than God. Somehow I believe that a life without temptation would be better and that I don't need the tests he allows me to pass through in order to be ready for whatever is next. Come to think of it, that mind-set entails surrender to each of the temptations—to provide for my own needs, to protect myself from danger, to exalt myself as lord.

When I pulled my new brother in Christ from the baptismal waters and heard his white robe sloshing around as he descended the steps from the baptistery, I was almost immediately embarrassed. I was ashamed of squirming at his expression of incredulity earlier. Yes, he used the Lord's name, but there was nothing vain about it.

He took my words with their full force, something I'd lost from repeating them so often. He was marching from those waters to fight the Devil, just as his Lord had done. And sensing something of what he was up against, he did precisely what his Bible prophesied about his Christ thousands of years before: "He shall cry to me, 'You are my Father, my God, and the Rock of my salvation'" (Ps. 89:26).

That's really what this book is about. I want you to see how imperiled you are. I want you to see how fought for you are. And I want you to be prompted to drop the book and pray to the only One who knows how to "destroy the works of the devil" (1 John 3:8). And I want to remember to do that too.

Oh my God.

NOTES

CHAPTER 1: WRESTLING WITH DEMONS

1. David Popenoe, *Families without Fathers: Fathers, Marriage and Children in American Society* (New Brunswick, NJ: Transaction, 2009), 140–150.

2. Barbara Brown Taylor, *Leaving Church: A Memoir of Faith* (New York: HarperCollins, 2006), 172.

CHAPTER 2: SLAUGHTERHOUSE DRIVE

1. "Killing with Kindness," *Driveway Moments: Radio Stories That Won't Let You Go* (National Public Radio, 2003), track 2.

2. Temple Grandin and Catherine Johnson, *Animals in Transition: Using the Mysteries of Autism to Decode Animal Behavior* (Orlando: Harcourt, 2005), 44–45.

3. John Chrysostom, "Homily XIII," in *Saint Chrysostom: Homilies on the Gospel of St. Matthew*, trans. G. Prevost, rev. M. Riddle, Nicene and Post-Nicene Fathers, First Series, Vol. 10 (Buffalo: Christian Literature, 1888; reprint, Grand Rapids, MI: Eerdmans, 1983), 81.

4. Maximus the Confessor, *On the Cosmic Mystery of Jesus Christ*, trans. Paul M. Bowers and Robert Louis Wilken (Crestwood, NY: St. Vladimir's Seminary Press, 2003), 111.

5. This statement is not without qualification. Sometimes we lash out the most fiercely at the very sins we commit (Rom. 2:21–23).

6. Thomas F. Torrance, *Incarnation: The Person and Life of Christ*, ed. Robert T. Walker (Downers Grove, IL: InterVarsity), 119.

7. Wendell Berry, *Life Is a Miracle: An Essay Against Modern Superstition* (Washington, DC: Counterpoint, 2000), 116.

8. Temple Grandin and Catherine Johnson, *Animals Make Us Human: Creating the Best Life for Animals* (Boston: Houghton Mifflin Harcourt, 2009), 299–300.

CHAPTER 3: STARVING TO DEATH

1. Leon R. Kass, *The Beginning of Wisdom: Reading Genesis* (New York: Free Press, 2003), 81.

2. Frederick Buechner, *Wishful Thinking: A Seeker's ABC*, revised and expanded (San Francisco: Harper, 1993), 65.

3. William B. Irvine, *A Guide to the Good Life: The Ancient Art of Stoic Joy* (New York: Oxford University Press, 2009), 65–84.

4. Mary Eberstadt, "The Weight of Smut," *First Things* (June/July 2010): 47–52.

5. In thinking this through in an American context, a good place to start is David Platt's piercingly convicting and exquisitely biblical book *Radical: Taking Back Your Faith from the American Dream* (Sisters, OR: Multnomah, 2010).

6. This line is attributed to Kate Michelman, formerly of the National Abortion Rights Action League. Elizabeth Achtemeier cites it in an address to the Presbyterians Pro-Life meeting at the General Assembly of the Presbyterian Church (USA), June 3, 1993.

7. For a prophetic critique of this phenomenon, see Ronald J. Sider, *The Scandal of the Evangelical Conscience: Why Are Christians Living Just Like the Rest of the World?* (Grand Rapids, MI: Baker, 2005), 17–35.

8. For an excellent analysis of these trends, see W. Bradford Wilcox, "Conservative Protestants and the Family: Resisting, Engaging, or Accommodating Modernity," in *A Public Faith: Evangelicals and Civic Engagement*, ed. Michael Cromartie (Lanham, MD: Rowman and Littlefield, 2003), 58.

9. Joseph Heath and Andrew Potter, *Nation of Rebels: Why Counterculture Became Consumer Culture* (San Francisco: Harper, 2004), 322.

10. David Wallis, "Questions for Ralph Nader: Give Them the Business," *New York Times Magazine*, June 16, 2002, 13.

11. John Updike, "How to Love America and Leave It at the Same Time," in *The Early Stories, 1953–1975* (New York: Alfred A. Knopf, 2003), 413.

12. Jeff Sharlet, *The Family: The Secret Fundamentalism at the Heart of American Power* (New York: Harper, 2009), 305.

13. Wendell Berry, "Inverting the Economic Order," *The Progressive* (September 2009), 19.

CHAPTER 4: FREE FALLING

1. Matthew ordered this temptation second in the flow of his narrative, while Luke ordered it third. For the sake of our discussion, we'll call it the second temptation here.

2. For a contemporary discussion of this phenomenon, which some of the fathers called "acedia," see Kathleen Norris, *Acedia and Me: A Marriage, Monks, and a Writer's Life* (New York: Riverhead, 2008).

3. Joyce G. Baldwin, *1 and 2 Samuel*, Tyndale Old Testament Commentary (Downers Grove, IL: InterVarsity, 1988), 295.

4. John Calvin, *Institutes of the Christian Religion* 3.51, trans. Ford Lewis Battles, ed. John T. McNeill (Philadelphia: Westminster, 1960), 919.

5. Patrick Henry Reardon, "Homer, Sex, and Bungee Jumping," *Touchstone: A Journal of Mere Christianity* (October 2003), 19.

6. Karl Barth, *Church Dogmatics*, vol. 2.1, *The Doctrine of God*, ed. G. W. Bromiley and T. F. Torrance (Edinburgh: T&T Clark, 1957), 641.

7. John M. Frame, *The Doctrine of God: A Theology of Lordship* (Phillipsburg, NJ: P&R, 2002), 595.

8. C. S. Lewis, *Mere Christianity* (New York: Macmillan, 1952; reprint, New York: HarperCollins, 2001), 52.

9. Thomas Merton, *Conjectures of a Guilty Bystander* (New York: Doubleday, 1966), 78.

10. Alan Wolfe, "The Culture War That Never Came," in *Is There a Culture War? A Dialogue on Values and American Public Life* (Washington, DC: Brookings Institution Press, 2006), 56.

11. William Faulkner, *The Wild Palms: [If I Forget Thee, Jerusalem]* (New York: Random House, 1939; reprint, New York: Vintage, 1995), 21.

CHAPTER 5: DESERT REIGN

1. Manya A. Brachear, "Satanist Puts Faith in System," *Chicago Tribune*, July 9, 2008, 3.

2. Florence King, *Reflections in a Jaundiced Eye* (New York: St. Martin's, 1989), 152.

3. William B. Irvine, *On Desire: Why We Want What We Want* (New York: Oxford University Press, 2006), 31.

4. David Brooks, "The Gospel of Mel Gibson," *New York Times*, July 16, 2010, A27.

Chapter 6: Where the Wild Things Aren't

1. Maurice Sendak, *Where the Wild Things Are* (New York: HarperCollins, 1963).

2. David Mills, "Enchanting Children," *Touchstone: A Journal of Mere Christianity* (December 2006), 21.

3. For an excellent defense of the warning passages as a means of endurance in the faith, see Thomas R. Schreiner, *Run to Win the Prize: Perseverance in the New Testament* (Wheaton, IL: Crossway, 2010).

4. Letter from Flannery O'Connor to Betty Hester, cited in Brad Gooch, *Flannery: A Life of Flannery O'Connor* (New York: Little, Brown, 2009), 337, from Flannery O'Connor, *Collected Works* (New York: Library of America, 1988), 948.

5. Selma G. Lanes, *The Art of Maurice Sendak* (New York: Abrams, 2003), 104.

Scripture Index

GENERAL INDEX

passions, 47
patience, 189
peace, 184, 188
persecution, 159
Peter, 113
political economy, 92–93
politics, 154–55
polygamy, 18
pornography, 83–84
Potter, Andrew, 90
power, 130, 140, 151, 160
prayer, 108, 111, 144, 146–47, 171
pride, 130, 133–34, 141–45, 148, 173–74
protection, 102–7, 112, 118, 126

rape, 18
Reardon, Patrick Henry, 114
redemption, 76, 169, 189
redemption plan, 29–30
repentance, 31, 84, 107, 148, 157, 167–68, 174, 188
revivals, 109–10
risks, 114–15

salvation, 75
sanctification, 107–8, 181
Satan
    as accuser, 140
    depictions of, 19, 139
    desires of, 46, 71
    exile of, 133–34, 137
    kingdom of, 141, 151
    power of, 160–61
    promises of, 132–33
    and use of Scripture, 99–101, 175
    worship of, 129–30, 142
    See also Devil; Serpent
satisfaction, 79
Saul, 118–19, 132–33, 142
Scripture, 182–83
self-control, 87, 94, 178, 181
self-exaltation, 144–47, 160
self-protection, 109, 111
self-provision, 63, 79, 94, 113–14
self-vindication, 121–22, 126
Serpent, 29, 38–39, 50–53, 64
sex, 82–83
sexual anarchy, 18
sexual infidelity, 83
signs, 104–5, 109–11, 117–18
sin
    and death, 50, 54
    exposure of, 173–74
    incited by Satan, 140

and prayerlessness, 171–72
and righteousness, 43–45, 155–56
slavery, 155
social justice, 154–55
Solomon, 133
sovereignty, 105, 135
suffering, 24, 126
sympathy, 44–45
syncretism, 142

Taylor, Barbara Brown, 24
temple, 99–100
temptation
    being aware of, 59
    to exalt yourself, 20–21, 28–29
    exposure of, 174–76
    and "getting caught", 57
    God's role in, 39–40, 184
    gradual path of, 27
    illusions of, 73
    lure of, 28
    overcoming, 22–23
    power of, 20, 22
    resisting of, 166, 170, 175, 177–78, 181, 184, 187
    as subtle, 48
    warnings of, 186
testing, 39–40, 103–6
theism, 134–35
Trinity, 135

unbelief, 104, 110

wealth, 86–87
wilderness, 52–54, 56, 59, 69–70, 76, 116, 141, 164
wisdom, 38, 48–49, 74, 133–36, 175, 183
worry, 146
worship, 91, 136–51, 189
worship wars, 149–50
wrath, 54